The Cocktail Keeper:
Recipes and Stories

by

Paul M. Markis

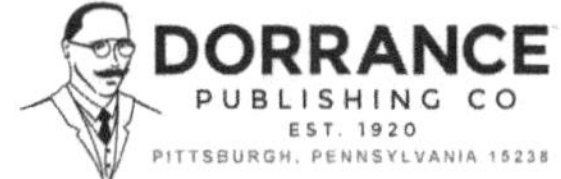
DORRANCE
PUBLISHING CO
EST. 1920
PITTSBURGH, PENNSYLVANIA 15238

Dorrance Publishing Co
585 Alpha Drive
Pittsburgh, PA 15238
Visit our website at www.dorrancebookstore.com

ISBN: 979-8-88925-413-3
eISBN: 979-8-88925-913-8

COCKTAIL KEEPER:
RECIPES and STORIES

This book is packed with:
cocktail recipes
real life industry stories
trivia
medicinal cures
famous toasts
helpful hints on drink making
lessons learned
quips and quotes
cocktail histories
techniques
special occasion menus
and so much more ...

About the Book:

I went to a bookstore and looked at existing cocktail books – many had some good points, but none were a one stop, practical book. Many had advice from business professionals, but almost none had stories about the people and places of the business. So that got me thinking: let me gather all this information and put it in a format that will appeal to an audience that bridges the home and professional bartender. Let me combine my casual writing style with my bar knowledge and create *The Cocktail Keeper: Recipes and Stories*, which is a good read with interesting facts and quips and makes it easy to create menus for almost every event and season.

The key to my recipes is simplicity, and this is for a few reasons. I want to make cocktails that are delicious, creative, somewhat trendy, and appeal to a wide range of customers. At the same time, the cocktails need to have minimal steps to mix so that the bartender is not overwhelmed, especially during busy times.

Every time a season changes, a holiday approaches, or an event is planned, there is always a scurry to look up related cocktail recipes, games, etc. Why not break the book down by traditional alphabetical cocktail recipe, but also cross reference by event menu? and sure, there are always new methods, spirits, and trends, but there are also some tried and true recipes that survive the ages.

Moreover, I created a collection of short stories that will be shared throughout the book. Readers will be able to get quick insights of the Americana feel to the restaurant business. Stories that you can relate to, that can be read at your own pace, and that you want to continue to read. Stories that will have you laughing, crying, or just scratching your head.

There are pictures of cocktails, but not every cocktail. There is a history of some cocktails, but not every cocktail. Quips and suggestions are dispersed throughout the book. It is not overloaded with coffee or tropical drinks, but just enough of each to satisfy everyone. There is a collection of famous toasts, but not so many that you can't remember them. There is even a section dedicated to medicinal cures.

Story 1 – *No One Had a Name*

I was 16 years old when I got my first restaurant job – I was a side cook and all-around errand boy. It was a cigarette smoke-filled neighborhood bar and grill. The food was some of the best around. This place won Boston's best several times. Hanging in the prep cooler was the giant side of beef and a lamb quarter. From these, they cut their own steak tips and lamb. They made their own burgers and sausage too.

This was a great neighborhood place, everyone- both workers and customers- all knew each other and their families. Most of them grew up in the area all their life. The only odd thing was that many did not have real names. There was Fuzzy, Fitzy, Butchy, Red Eye, Ski, Beau Beau, Two Toes, Lefty, Porka, Mac, JB, and so many more. They used these pseudonyms exclusively, so I never got to know their real names. When Ski passed away I didn't even know it because I never knew his real name!

They all had wild stories of their crazy younger days. and this was the perfect place for them. The only window in the place was a peep hole in the front door, kind of like an open to the public speakeasy.

My parents didn't like that I worked there. They didn't want me to be involved in any of the occasional gambling and stuff that went on. I guess they didn't want me to pick up any bad habits. and I would always smell like cigarette smoke. The customers were big time chain smokers. But all in all, my parents knew those guys would keep an eye on me and make sure I didn't get in any trouble ... usually! and it was a pretty popular and respected restaurant. In time they all became my second family.

This was also my first exposure to the "three martini lunch." Being close to the airport, we had many of the airfreight salesmen conducting business as they were dining their clients. I always thought a martini was a wimpy drink because these guy would drink them down and then go back to work!

When I was in college, they let me bartend. The guys at the bar drank mostly beer and liquor on the rocks. Their wives would have wine when they came in for dinner on the weekends. It was a pretty boring gig. I convinced the owner let me hang a drink of the day special, just to get used to making different drinks, which I thought was nice of him. Nothing too exciting, just drinks like a Cape Codder or Screwdriver. I worked a lunch shift and had to master martini making – man, my whole outlook on the martini changed. I thought, how do these guys drink three of these and return to finish off the rest of the work day?

The movie "Cocktail" was just out and cocktails were popular. The guys always wanted me to toss the bottles around. and I did very limited juggling of bottles. Especially when the owner allowed me to on one condition – any bottle that broke I had to pay for ... that put an end to my bottle tossing skills.

With the encouragement of the bar customers, I asked for a raise. The minimum at the time was $3.25, so I asked the owner for $7 an hour ... to which, without missing a beat, he replied, "Sure, what hour?"

I loved that place and everyone there.

To this day sometimes I still answer the phone, "Hello, Barney's."

LESSON LEARNED: The first place is always the best place ... Thanks for the memories.

Glassware

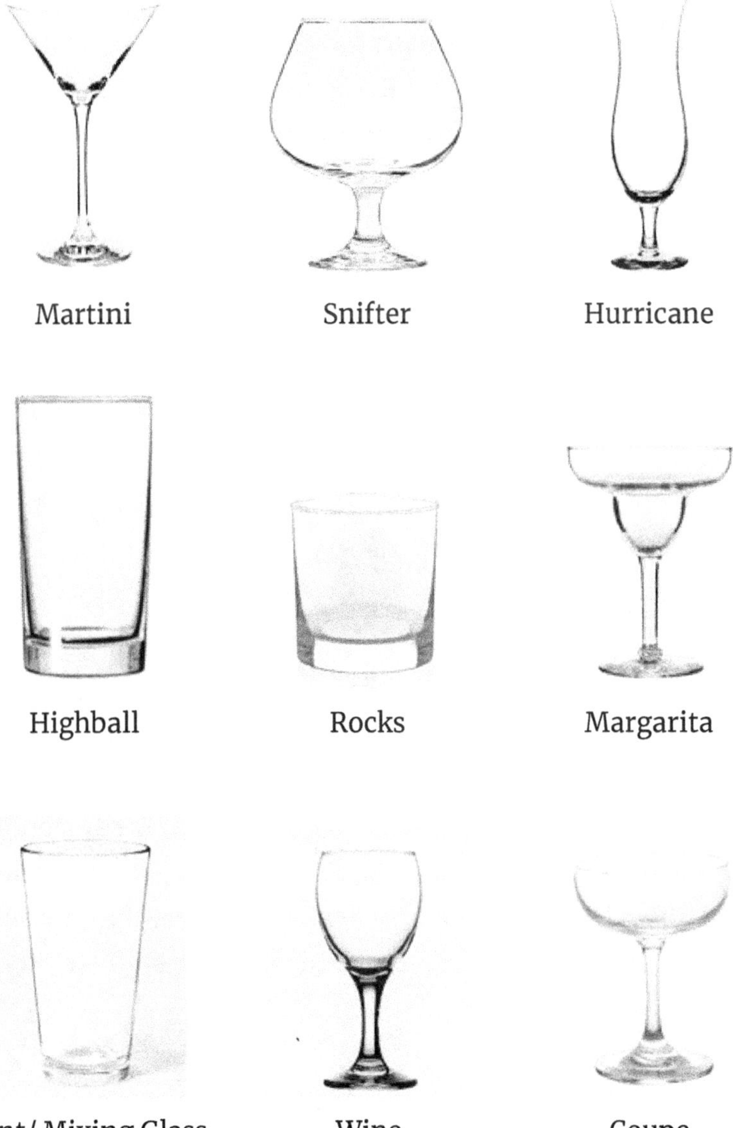

Martini

Snifter

Hurricane

Highball

Rocks

Margarita

Pint/ Mixing Glass

Wine

Coupe

SOME ADVICE ON SERVICE

Take it for what it's worth; everyone finds their own balance. Service workers that do well in the industry are professionals and do a lot of the following by habit. Customers appreciate a well-managed table and have a better experience because of it.

Be the Show

As the bartender and even a server, you need to make a presentation like it's the best thing in the world. The food tastes so much better if its presented to the customer in a regal manner. Food is enjoyed with all the senses. The same goes for cocktails; mix the drink with purpose. Your work should attract the eyes of customers. Be a showman; you'll make more tips because customers will have a great experience.

Acknowledge the Customers

Sometimes we just get so busy that you can't get to everyone in a timely manner. It is important that you at least acknowledge them and assure them that you will be with them asap. Eye contact and a nod mean a lot. No one likes to be ignored! Even if someone is waiting a while for their cocktail, be sure that when it's their turn you make them feel like a king or queen, like they are the only ones that matter to you. They'll forget the wait and have smiles on their faces.

"Read the Table"

Figure out what type of customer you have. Are they in a rush? Do they need help having a good time? Are they needy? Figure out what you need to do and say to make sure they have an exceptional experience. Some people you can fool around with, some people you can't. Are they drinkers? Are they foodies? Remember, you are managing the table.

Be Aware of Your Customers

Make sure your customers get good service. Have benchmarks for yourself. Visit them at least five times during their stay. Start with a cocktail right away and ask if they want to try a special/appetizer.

Be aware of the guests' needs and remember timing is everything. offer wine or beer before their entrees arrive. offer them dessert/dessert drinks/coffee drinks after their meal. If you see their cocktail down to only a quarter, ask if they would like to enjoy another cocktail.

Treat All Customers Well

Sure, it's always good to take care of your regular customers well, and you should know what level of service they like. But don't do it at the expense of new or occasional customers. Treating everyone with quality service that fulfills their expectations will help the house and you make extra money. Take the opportunity to build a return customer base. Don't be that person who only gives good service to the regulars; be welcoming to all. Make everyone feel like a regular customer.

Banana Nutbread

Bunny Bowl

Black Cat Martini

Blackberry Bourbon Sidecar

Blackberry Smash

COCKTAIL KEEPER

Before we start: Drink Mixers are important:

Always use good quality mixers, especially if it's a component of the cocktail. So in a Cape Codder you may want a quality cranberry juice because it's a big part of the drink. a good example here is to use light cream in a White Russian; you may not want to kill the customer with heavy cream, and, conversely, milk may be too light. It really does taste so much richer with the light cream. Don't skimp in this area – It will throw off the whole flavor component.

A

Agave E Limone
>1.5 Oz Tequila
>½ Oz Fresh Lime Juice
>½ Oz Fresh Lemon Juice
>¾ Oz Pineapple Juice
>½ Oz Agave Syrup
>½ Oz Burrata Water

Coupe
Big ice cube in a shaker, for 10-15 seconds, double strain in a coupe glass and top w/ dehydrated lemon, and salt

All American
>1.5 Oz Bourbon
>1 Oz Amaretto
>Splash Simple Syrup
>Fill With Apple Cider

Cocktail/Martini

Alabama Slammer
>1.5 Oz Southern Comfort
>½ Oz Amaretto
>½ Oz Sloe Gin
>Fill With Orange Juice
>Garnish With Cherry and Orange Slice

Cocktail
Donette's favorite – a great customer/friend

Al Capone — Cocktail

- 1.5 Oz Whiskey
- 1 Oz Campari
- .5 Oz Sweet Vermouth
- Splash of Soda Water

Aloha Delight — Cocktail

- 1 Oz Brandy
- 1 Oz Vodka
- Pineapple Juice
- Orange Juice
- Garnish With Cherry and Pineapple

Aperolgroni — Rocks

- 1.5 Oz Gin
- .5 Oz Dry Vermouth
- .5 Oz Aperol
- Splash of Grapefruit Juice

Aperol Manhattan — Martini

- 2 Oz Bourbon
- ¾ Oz Aperol
- ¾ Oz Sweet Vermouth
- Splash of ¼ Oz Simple Syrup
- Garnish with Cherries

Apple Pie Martini — Martini

- 1.5 Oz Vanilla Vodka
- Fill with Apple Cider
- Cinnamon Stick
- Sugar Cinnamon Rimmed Glass

Apple Sauce Martini   Martini
    2.5 Oz Apple Pucker
    .5 Oz Cinnamon Schnapps
    Fill With Pineapple Juice
    Sugar Rimmed Glass

Appletini   Martini
    2.5 Oz Vodka
    1 Oz Apple Pucker
    Splash of Sour Mix
    Garnish: Cherry

Remember: always fill the glass or shaker (mixer glass) with ice. The liquids will usually reach the top of any glass. If you shake or stir the cocktail/martini and strain it into a glass filled with ice, it should come out in near perfect amounts. Have some fun with it – play around with measurements to get your desired flavor. In time, your hands will know the measures.

Apple Cider Cinnamon Sangria   Wine
    3 Oz White Wine
    2 Oz Apple Cider
    1.5 Oz Workingman's Distillery Cinnamon Whiskey
    Served over ice in a wine glass with cinnamon sugar rim
    cinnamon stick and apple chunks.

Apricot Spritz   Wine
    1.5 Oz Apricot Vodka
    3 Oz Prosecco
    Served On Ice In A Wine Glass

Apricot-Rosemary Mimosa   Wine Glass
    1.5 Oz Apricot Vodka
    3 Oz Prosecco
    Over Ice In a Wine Glass
    Splash of Simple Syrup
    Garnish With Sprig of Rosemary

Arnold Palmer's 19th Hole   Cocktail
    1.5 Oz Don Q Rum   *Named for the great golf*
    Lemonade and Iced Tea   *pro. You should know that*
the 19th hole is the
Clubhouse !

Arugulito   Rocks
    2 Oz Bombay Saffire Gin
    Splash of Simple Syrup
    Muddled Arugula and Lime
    Garnish with Arugula and Lime Wedge

Aye Coolcumber   Cocktail
    1.5 Oz Hendricks Gin   *Hendricks is infused with*
    Top Off with Soda Water   *cucumber and rose. A drop*
    Splash of Simple Syrup   *of rose water or a rose*
    Muddled Cucumber   *petal garnish will make*
    Garnish: Cucumber Slice   *this drink pop.*

To LAYER a drink means to float one spirit on top of the other. You have to do this slow and gentle to keep them separated.

I find it best to pour the first layer, then pour the second layer slowly over the back of a spoon to gently slide it in and make it float on top of the previous pour. Repeat until all layers are completed. of course lighter spirits on top of the heavier one.

To "FLOAT" means after the cocktail is mixed and poured into the glass, gently pour the float spirit on top. This is usually a darker rum that is actually lighter bodied and stays floating on top for a while giving a nice look. Two cocktails that come to mind using this technique are Bahama Mama and Screaming Viking.

B

B-52   Shot
    (Layered Drink)
    ¾ Oz Kahlua
    ½ Oz Baileys
    ½ Oz Grand Marnier

Bahama Mama   Cocktail
    1.5 Oz Coconut Rum
    Orange and Pineapple Juices
    Splash of Grenadine
    Float of Gosling Black Seal Rum

Banana Nut Bread   Rocks
    1.5 Oz Cream De Banana   *Tastes just like my Aunt*
    Splash of ¾ Oz Frangelico   *Norma's banana nut bread.*
    Splash of Light Cream   *Close my eyes memories.*
    Graham Cracker Rimmed Glass

Banana Banshee   Pint Beer Glass
    1.5 Oz Cream De Banana   Shake Up
    ½ Oz White Cream De Cocoa
    1 Oz Vanilla Vodka
    Ice Cream Mix
    Top With Whipped Cream
    Banana Chips

Bay Breeze   Cocktail
    (Also Called a Hawaiian Seabreeze)
    1.5 Oz Vodka
    Half Cranberry Juice
    Half Pineapple Juice
    Garnish With a Pineapple Chunk and Cherry

Bayou Bloody Mary	Pint

    1.5 Oz Vodka
    Bloody Mary Mix
    Cajun Spices
    A Dash of Hot Sauce
    Garnish With a Cajun Grilled Shrimp

Beam Me Up Scottie	Shot

    ½ Oz Kahlua
    ½ Oz Banana Liquor
    ½ Oz Baileys
    Dash of Frangelico

Beachcomber	Cocktail

    1 Oz Bacardi Rum
    1 Oz Myers Dark Rum
    1 Oz Triple Sec
    Lemon Juice
    Simple Syrup
    Dash of Grenadine

Between the Sheets	Cocktail

    1.5 Oz Brandy
    ¾ Oz Rum
    ¾ Oz Triple Sec
    Sour Mix

Big Banana	Margarita

    1 Oz Bacardi Rum
    1 Oz Goslings Dark Rum
    ¾ Oz Creme De Banana
    Splash of Light Cream
    Shake Well

Bit a Bittah — Rocks
    1.5 Oz Reyka Vodka
    House Made Grapefruit Balsamic Syrup
    Splash of Grenadine
    Splash of Campari
    Garnish: Lemon Wheel

Black Cat Martini — Martini
    2.5 Oz Reyka Vodka
    1 Oz Blackberry Brandy
    Splash of Blue Curacao

Blackberry Bourbon Sidecar — Cocktail
    1.5 Oz Woodford Reserve Bourbon
    ½ oz Cointreau
    Soda Water
    Muddled Blackberries
    Garnish With Thyme

Just a wonderful cocktail – it's a trendy bourbon cocktail and fresh fruit combination. It really does excite the senses.

Blackberry Margarita — Margarita
    1.5 Oz Tequila
    ¾ Oz Triple Sec
    Agave
    Muddled Blackberries
    Splash of Sour Mix
    Garnish With Blackberries

When muddling, I find it best to do it in the mixing container – you are smashing the fruit and herbs just enough to release the oils – then add your spirits and mix, but you don't want all that broken fruit and herbs in the cocktail (it will look pretty bad!) so use a strainer to STRAIN it into the cocktail glass then garnish with other whole fruit and herbs.

Blackberry Smash

COCKTAIL

    1.5 Oz Don Q Rum
    Muddled Blackberries and Mint
    Fill With Ginger Beer
    Strained
    Garnish With Blackberries and Mint

Black Fig Martini

MARTINI

It helps if you have the flavored vodka but you can always infuse your own.

    2.5 Oz Black Fig Vodka
    1 Oz Reyka Vodka
    Cranberry Juice
    Garnish With a Figlet (If Available)

Black Forest Cake

FROZEN/Shakeup

    1.5 Oz Vodka
    ½ Oz Chambord
    ½ Oz Kahlua
    Ice Cream

Blue Hawaii

FROZEN

    1.5 Oz Rum
    Pineapple Juice
    ¼ Oz Blue Curacao
    Cream De Coconut
    Garnish With Pineapple and Cherry

Blue Lagoon

MARTINI

Just a tiny splash of blue curacao. Reyka is a vodka from Iceland made from the melting glacier water and naturally filtered through a lava field thus the name Blue Lagoon.

    2 .5 Oz Reyka Icelandic Vodka
    Lemonade
    Splash of blue curacao

Blow Job
    ½ Oz Kahlua
    ½ Oz Amaretto
    ½ Oz Baileys
    Whipped Cream

PONY/Shot Glass

Blueberry Martini
    2.5 Oz Cold River Blueberry Vodka
    Lemonade
    Splash of Sprite
    Splash of Blue Curacao
    Garnish With Blueberries If Available

MARTINI
This is an amazing potato vodka–the aroma of wild blueberries will fill the room. Distilled in Maine of course.

(The) Bookmaker
    1.5 Oz Strega
    ¾ Oz Fresh Lime Juice
    1 Oz Pineapple Juice
    ¾ Oz Vanilla Syrup
    Garnish With Dehydrated Lemon

COCKTAIL
Whip, shake, and double strain over a big ice cube.

Bootleggers Negrone
    2.5 Oz Bourbon
    ½ Oz Campari
    ½ Oz Triple Sec
    Orange Bitters

MARTINI

Bourbon Old Fashion
    1.5 Oz Woodford Reserve Bourbon
    Soda Water
    Raw Sugar
    A Few Dashes of Bitters
    Served Over an Ice Sphere
    Garnished with a Cherry and Orange Slice

ROCKS
Any bourbon is fine – but you should know that Woodford is the preferred bourbon of Kentucky Derby.

To make a PUREE is fairly easy. In a blender, combine the ingredients – usually fresh fruit and simple syrup or juice – pour the simple syrup to the top of the fruit , this will give you a good measure – then mix until smooth as possible. I then transfer it to a squeeze bottle so it's easy to use.

Bramble Bay Martini
    2.5 Oz Malfy Italian Gin
    House Made Raspberry/
    Blackberry Puree

Martini
Try making your own purees Easy – blend fresh fruit and simple syrup

Brandy Alexander
    1.5 Oz House Brandy
    1 Oz Dark Cream De Cocoa
    Splash of Light Cream
    Served On Ice

Snifter/Rocks
Whenever I feel a cold coming on have a few of these before bedtime and you'll wake up feeling much better.

Brandy Float
    1.5 Oz White Creme De Menthe (Chilled)
    Float of Brandy

Bikini Martini
    2.5 Oz Don Q Coconut Rum
    Pineapple Juice
    Splash of Grenadine

Martini

Blackberry Margarita
    1.5 Oz Agavalez Tequila
    3/4 Oz Triple Sec
    Agave
    Muddled Blackberries
    Splash of Sour Mix
    Garnished With Blackberries

Margarita

Bloody Mary
    1.5 Oz Vodka
    Bloody Mary Mix
    Horseradish
    your taste –
    Red Hot Sauce

Pint
Get a good quality and tasting mix, you may have to bring it to keep track of what you add for consistency.

Bloody Maria
    1.5 Oz Tequila
    Tomato Juice
    Red Hot Sauce
    Horseradish
    Red Pepper Flakes

Pint

Blueberry Martini
    2.5 Oz Cold River
    Blueberry Vodka
    Blueberry Juice Or Puree
    Splash of Lemonade
    Sprite
    Garnish with Blueberries (If Available)

Martini
This is a good example of supporting a regional/local company distillery. Cold river distilleries and it's an awesome flavor and from Maine.

Blue Collar Bourbon Smash
    1.5 Oz Blue Collar Bourbon
    Splash of Soda Water

Rocks
Blue Collar Bourbon is an example of a local distillery

Muddled Mint and Peaches
    ½ Oz Triple Sec
    Simple Syrup
    Garnish With a Mint Leaf

Working Man's Distillery located In North Attleborough, MA great products and creative cocktails

Boston Strong
    2.5 Oz Bully Boy Whiskey Distilled
    1 Oz Sweet Vermouth
    Garnish With Cranberries

Manhattan
We made this after the marathon bombing. in Boston

Bourbon Revival — Rocks
    1.5 Oz Elijah Craig Bourbon
    Blood Orange Mixer
    ¾ Oz Lillett Blanc
    Squeeze of Lemon Juice
    Orange Wheel Garnish

I Heard About This From a Bar Friend – James. He Placed In a Spirits Contest With This. I Made a Few Adjustments… a Bar Favorite.

Boulevardier — Cocktail
    1.5 Oz Bourbon
    ¾ Oz Campari
    ¾ Oz Sweet Vermouth

Brave Bull — Shot
    1 Oz Tequila
    ¾ Oz Kahlua

Bubbly — Martini
    2.5 Oz Malfy Italian Gin
    Prosecco
    Topped With Simple Syrup
    Garnish With Lemon Wheel

Keep It Local

Try to have as many local products as possible. There are lots of local breweries and distilleries, so make sure you have some of their product, even if you have to make special cocktails with them. People like to support the local establishments. Today, there are usually breweries and distilleries in a ten mile radius of wherever your place is. All of New England would be considered local, and there are lots of offerings from those 6 states. Don't be afraid to get a really good spirit or beer from Maine or Vermont. and don't forget, there are lots of local wineries making fruit-based wine year round.

Bucca Blast

    ¾ Oz Black Sambucca

    ¾ Oz Vodka

Shot

Bullied Apple Martini

    1.5 Oz Bully Boy Whiskey

    1 Oz Apple Pucker

    Cranberry Juice

Martini

A Play On The Washington Apple But Using Bully Boy Whiskey Distilled In Boston.

Bullied Berry

    1.5 Oz Bully Boy Whiskey

    Ginger Ale

    Float of Blackberry Brandy

    Served Over Ice

    Garnish With Orange Wheel

Rocks

Bully Boy Is Distilled In Boston and Has A Wide Range of Spirits.

Bunny Bowl

    ¾ Oz Stoli Vanilla Vodka

    ¾ oz Irish Cream

    Splash of Dorda Chocolate Liquor

    Served in a bunny

Chocolate Bunny

Dark cream de cacao works well also, but you really need a chocolate bunny. Cut off the ears and use the hollow bunny body as the glass.

Butterball

    ¾ Oz Butterscotch Schnapps

    ¾ Oz Baileys

Shot

Butter Cup

    1 Oz Butterscotch Schnapps

    Hot Chocolate

    Whipped Cream

Mug

Buttered Popcorn

    1.5 Oz Tullamore Dew (Rum Cask)

    1 Oz Butterscotch Schnapps

Rocks

No substitutes – it really does taste like buttered popcorn!

Buttershot

    1.5 Oz Bulleit Bourbon

    1 Oz Butterscotch Schnapps

    Bitters

    Muddled Cherries

Old Fashion

Buzzards Bay Breeze

    1.5 Oz Great White Rum

    Pineapple Juice

    Cranberry Juice

    Garnish with Lime

Cocktail

You can use any rum but keeping with the name. I chose to use a brand from Cape Cod Distillery.

Cape Codder

Chocolate Shake Up

Eve's Temptation

C

Candy Cane   Martini
  2.5 Oz Peppermint Schnapps
  Light Cream
  Garnish With a Red Sugar Rim
  Garnish With Candy Cane

Cantaloupe Martini — Martini
2.5 Oz Don Q Rum
Muddled Blackberries and Mint
Cantaloupe Puree
Garnish With a Cantaloupe Melon Ball

Capri Royale Martini — Martini
2 Oz Limoncello
Prosecco

Captain's Bounty — Cocktail
1.5 Oz Captain Morgan Spiced Rum
Ginger Ale

A little different, but really nice.

Cappuccino Martini — Martini
1.5 Oz Baileys Espresso Cream
1 Oz Stoli Vanilla Vodka
½ Oz Dark Cream De Cocoa
Splash of Light Cream
Dusting of Cocoa Powder

Cape Mandarin — Cocktail
1.5 Oz Mandarin Vodka
Soda Water
Splash of Cranberry Juice

Cape Codder Cocktail — Cocktail
1.5 Oz Cape Cod Vodka
Soda Water
Cranberry Juice
Red Sugar Rimmed Glass
Garnish With Cranberries

A Massachusetts distillery based in Massapee, MA. Turn this into a special around the cranberry harvest in Sept/Oct.

Carnival Punch Hurricane
  1.5 Oz Vodka
  1 Oz Pama Pomegranate Liquor
  Pineapple Juice
  Squeeze of Lemon, and Ginger Beer

Caribbean Coffee   Coffee Mug
  1oz Bacardi Rum   *A delight best known as the*
  1 Oz Kahlua   *official drink of the Mr. Markis*
  Top With Whipped Cream   *Holiday Fest.*

Carrot Cake   Rocks
  1.5 Oz Baileys   *This needs to be mixed just right*
  1 Oz Butterscotch Schnapps   *or else it'll taste like an oatmeal*
  ½ Oz Cinnamon Schnapps   *cookie. Play around with the*
  On The Rocks   *measurements you will know*
                                  when it's right!

Chalada Chill   Pint Beer Glass
  1.5 Oz Don Q Coconut Rum
  1 Oz Rum Chata
  Splash of Vanilla Vodka
  Iced Coffee

Chateau Coffee   Coffee
  1 Oz Rum Chata
  1 Oz Kahlua (Kamora)

Chocolate Candy   Martini
  1 Oz Peppermint Schnapps
  2.5 Oz White Chocolate Liquor
  Red Sugar Rimmed Glass

Chocolate Cake Shot   Shot
    ¾ Oz Citron (Lemon) Vodka
    ¾ Oz Frangelico
    Served On Rocks Or Chilled

Chocolate Chip Cookie / Muffin   Martini
    2 Oz Cookie Dough Vodka   *It Helps If You Have The Flavored*
    1 Oz Irish Cream Liquor   *Vodka!*
    Garnish With Chocolate Shaving
    Rimmed Glass

Chocolate Coconut Passion   Rocks
    1.5 Oz Dorda Chocolate Liquor
    1 Oz Spiced Coconut Cream Liquor
    Served On The Rocks

Chocolate Covered Cherry   Martini
    1.5 Oz Cherry Vodka
    1.5 Oz White Cream De Cocoa
    Red Sugar Rimmed Glass
    White Chocolate Covered Cherry

Chocolate Delight   Cocktail
    1.5 Oz Coconut Rum   *This is pretty close to a Chunky*
    1 Oz Banana Liquor   *Monkey. Makes a great frozen*
    Pineapple Juice   *drink too. Use a real banana,*
    Hershey Syrup   *throw it in the blender.*

Churchill Downs Cocktail   Cocktail
    1.5 Oz Markers Mark
    Ginger Ale
    Top With Blackberry Brandy
    Splash of Simple Syrup

Chocolate Martini — Martini
2.5 Oz Stoli Vanilla
¾ Oz Dark Cream De Cocoa
¾ Oz Dorda Chocolate Liquor
Splash of Light Cream
Coco Powder Rimmed Glass

Dorda is a nice thick chocolate liquor will add a nice flavor and texture

Chocolate Shake - Up — Pint Beer Glass or Mason Jar
1 Oz Dark Cream De Cocao
¾ Oz Vanilla Vodka
Splash of Dorda Chocolate Liquor
Ice Cream Mix / Light Cream
Top With Whipped Cream
Chocolate Chips Garnish

Christmas Cocktail — Cocktail
1.5 Oz Gin
¾ Oz Lillett Blanc
Splash ½ Oz of Simple Syrup
Top off With Cranberry Juice
Red Sugar Rimmed Glass

Chocolate Truffle — Mini Snifter
1.5 Oz Dorda Chocolate Liquor
Splash ½ Oz of Cointreau
Garnished With Chocolate Covered Orange
Straight Up *(No Ice)*
After Dinner Drink

Citrus Basil Tea — Rocks
Muddled Basil Leaves
2 Oz Rum
Iced Tea
Simple Syrup
Squeeze of Fresh Lemon Juice
Garnish With Lemon and Basil

Citrus Flower — Cocktail

1.5 Oz Deep Eddy Lemon Vodka
Cranberry and Orange Juice
Topped With a Float ½ Oz of St Elders

Contessa Cocktail — Cocktail

1.5 Oz Gin
¾ Oz Dry Vermouth
Splash ¼ Oz of Lillet Blanc
Squeeze of Fresh Lemon Juice

Clear Chocolate Martini — Martini

2.5 Oz Stoli Vanilla Vodka
1 Oz White Cream De Cocoa
Drop In Hershey Kisses
(If Available)

Although not verified, I have been told that vodka and white cream de cacao was the original White Russian.

Cosmopolitan — Martini

2.5 Oz Cytron Vodka
1 Oz Triple Sec Or Cointreau
Lime Juice
Top off With Cranberry Juice
Squeeze of Fresh Lime
Garnish: Lime Wedge

Lorraine always had it with cointreau!

Cotton Tail Marga-Tini — Rocks

1.5 Oz Tequila
¾ Oz Triple Sec
Coconut Milk
Pineapple and Lime Juice
Served Over Ice In a Rocks Glass
Marshmallow Fluff and Coconut Rim

Cotton Tail Martini   Martini
    1 Oz Stoli Vanilla Vodka
    1 Oz Whipped Cream Vodka
    Rim The Glass With Marshmallow
    Fluff and Coconut Flakes

Country Lemonade   Cocktail
    1.5 Oz Jim Beam Maple Bourbon   *As a substitute you can use bourbon*
    Soda Water   *with a splash of real maple syrup or*
    Lemonade   *on the light side substitute with*
                                       vodka

Creme Brulé Martini   Martini
    2.5 Oz Vanilla Vodka
    ¾ Oz Butterscotch Schnapps
    ½ Oz Baileys
    Garnish – Cinnamon Sprinkle

Creamsicle   Cocktail
    1.5 Oz Banana Liquor or Amaretto
    ¾ Oz Triple Sec
    Splash of Oj
    Light Cream

Cream Soda Cocktail   Cocktail
    Hard Root Beer
    1.5 Oz Marshmallow or Vanilla Vodka

Cuba Libre   Cocktail
    1.5 Oz White Rum
    Soda Water
    Coca-Cola
    Float of Goslings Black Seal Rum
    Squeeze of Lime
    Garnish With a Lime

Muddling

Muddling should not be a workout for the bartender, you're not at the gym. Muddling should be to only release the oils from the herbs or fruits, you do not have to mush it! Don't overwork it, it changes the flavor profile if you turn it to mush.

Cucumber Basil Gimlet

Rocks

1.5 Oz Reyka Vodka
Muddled Cucumber and Basil
Soda Water and Lemonade
Garnish: Cucumber Slice and
Basil Leaf

A crowd favorite – totally delicious the use of muddled herbs and cucumber adds a great flavor profile

Cucumber Margarita (Spicy)

Margarita

1.5 Oz Tequila
¾ Oz Triple Sec
Muddled Jalapeno and Cucumber
Splash of Sour Mix
Lime Juice

Cucumber Splash

Cocktail

Muddled Cucumbers
1.5 Oz Gin Lane
Ginger Beer
and Soda Water
Lime Juice

D

Dark and Stormy

Beer

Ginger Beer
Topped With Goslings Black
Seal Rum
Served Over Ice

So good on a stormy winter night allegedly got its name from an old sailor who compared the drink's murky hue to the color of storm clouds

Dirty Shirley
    1.5 Oz Cherry Vodka
    Ginger Ale Or Sprits
    Grenadine

Cocktail
Proof That Adults Can Have Soft Drinks

Dorda Truffle
    2 Oz Dorda Chocolate Liquor
    1 Oz Cointreau

Martini

Dr Pepper
    1.5 Oz Sloe Gin
    ¾ Oz Southern Comfort
    Coke

Cocktail

Dubonet Cocktail
    1.5 Oz Gin
    1 Oz Dubonet Wine
    Fill With Ice
    Garnish With Lemon Twist

Wine Glass

E

Eggnog
    1.5 Oz Maple Bourbon
    Eggnog
    Splash of Light Cream
    Nutmeg Rimmed Glass

Cocktail
Just one of many eggnog recipes many recipes use brandy – the beauty of this is it can be made individually – no need for a punch bowl.

Elderflower Fizz
    1.5 Oz St Elders
    Soda Water
    ¾ Oz Grappa
    Dash of Lime Juice
    Garnish With Grapes

Cocktail

El Diablo   Cocktail
    1.5 Oz Vodka
    Ginger Beer
    Splash of Blackberry Brandy

End of Summer Cocktail   Wine Glass
    1.5 Oz Gin Lane
    ¾ Oz Lillett Blanc
    ¾ Oz St Elders
    Pineapple Juice
    Splash of Simple Syrup
    Garnish With Cucumber Slice
    And Assorted Berries
    Served Over Ice In a Wine Glass

Espresso Martini   Martini
    Cold Espresso   *Please use real espresso – I make a*
    2.5 Oz Stoli Vanilla Vodka   *pot and keep it in refrigerator*
    Splash of Kamora/Kahlua
    Splash of Irish Cream Liquor

(Perfect) Espresso Martini   Martini
    Oz Vanilla Vodka
    1 Oz Coffee Liquor
    ½ Oz Vanilla Syrup
    Fill With Espresso
    Pinch of Salt

Espresso Italiano   Martini
    Espresso Coffee   *The Italian version of espresso*
    2.5 Oz Stoli Vanilla Vodka   *martini*
    Splash of Tia Maria
    Scoop of Vanilla Ice Cream

Eve's Temptation
    Apple Cider
    1.5 Oz Coconut Rum
    Cranberry Juice
    Splash of Cinnamon Schnapps
    Edible Glitter (Gold/Silver)
    Sugar Cinnamon Rimmed Glass
    Float a Blinking Light Ice Cube

Large Snifter
This is a pretty cocktail and the floating blinking ice cube is an attention – getter. It's worth time to get these cubes

F

Fall Bellini
    Prosecco
    1 Oz Black Fig Vodka
    1 Oz Apple Pucker
    Garnish With a Fig

Champagne Flute

Fall Harvest Sangria
    Red Wine (Sangiovese)
    Orange Juice and Sprite
    Top With Apple Pucker
    On The Rocks
    Orange and Cherry Garnish

Wine Glass

The Finish Line
    Oz Orange Vodka
    1 oz Triple Sec
    Orange and Cranberry Juices

Cocktail
Created to honor our business partner Troy–he ran 25 consecutive Boston marathons and counting.

Fireball
    ¾ Oz Cherry Brandy
    ¾ Oz Cinnamon Schnapps
    Dash of Tobasco

Shot

Fitfty-Seven (57) T-Bird   Cocktail
    ½ Oz Sloe Gin   *Car enthusiasts love these - travel*
    ½ Oz Gin   *all four states in one sitting!*
    ½ Oz Amaretto
    ½ Oz Southern Comfort
    Sour Mix
    Fl Plates – Orange Juice
    Ma Plates – Cranberry Juice
    Ha Plates – Pineapple Juice
    Ca Plates – Grapefruit Juice

Fog Cutter   Cocktail
    1 Oz Bacardi Rum
    1 Oz Brandy
    1 Oz Gin
    Sour Mix
    Orgeat
    Orange Juice
    Float of ¼ Oz Sherry

Frisky Whiskey   Rocks
    West Cork Irish Whiskey   *I just love the name of this cocktail*
    Orange Juice
    Splash of Simple Syrup
    Garnish: Orange Wheel

French Quarter   Cocktail
    Gin
    Aperol
    Sour Mix
    Prosecco

French Martini   Martini
    Grey Goose Vodka
    Chambord
    Pineapple Juice

French Toast Martini — Martini
  Rum Chata
  Jim Beam Maple Bourbon
  Cinnamon Sugar Rim

*It really does taste like French toast–
you can use any bourbon with a
splash of maple syrup.*

Front Porch Tea — Cocktail
  Bourbon, Peach Schnapps,
  Iced Tea, Over Ice
  Garnish With a Peach Slice

Fudgesicle — Frozen
  Kahlua
  Dark Creme De Cacao
  Light Cream/Ice Cream Mix

Fuzzy Navel — Cocktail
  Peach Schnapps
  Orange Juice

Gold Rush Hot Coco

Here's Looking At You Cosmo

G

Gimlet   Rocks
    Gin
    Lime Juice
    Fresh Squeezed Lime

Gin Ricky   Cocktail
    1.5 Oz Gin
    Soda Water
    Lime and Lime Juice

Gin Buck   Cocktail
    1.5 Oz Gin
    Ginger Ale

Gibson   Martini
    2.5 Oz Gin
    ¾ Oz Dry Vermouth
    Garnish With a Cocktail Onion

Gingerbread Martini   Martini
    1 Oz Gingerbread Cream Liquor
    1.5 Oz Captain Morgan
    Gingerbread Rimmed Glass
    Serve With a Ginger Snap

Girl Scout Cookie   Cocktail
    1 Oz Peppermint Schnapps
    Or Crème De Menthe
    1.5 Oz Dark Creme De Cacao
    Fill With Light Cream

Godfather   Rocks
    1.5 Oz Scotch (Dewars)
    1 Oz Amaretto

Godmother   Rocks
    1.5 Oz Vodka
    1 Oz Amaretto

Golden Dream   Cocktail
    1.5 Oz Galliano
    1 Oz Triple Sec
    Orange Juice
    Milk

Gold Rush Hot Coco   Coffee Mug
    Hot Cocoa Packet
    1.5 Oz Coconut Rum
    ¾ Oz Amaretto
    Topped With Whipped Cream
    A Sprinkle of Gold Leaf Sugar

No matter where you are, close your eyes and you'll feel like you're in front of a fireplace at a ski lodge.

Goom Bay Smash   Cocktail
    1.5 Oz Coconut Rum
    Orange Juice
    Pineapple Juice
    Dash of Grenadine
    Dash of Banana Liquor

Grateful Dead   Cocktail
    ¾ Oz Vodka   *Note: Many places do not serve*
    ¾ Oz Rum   *these or limit how many you can*
    ¾ Oz Gin   *have because of amount of*
    ¾ Oz Tequila   *liquor it contains*
    ½ Oz Triple Sec
    ½ Oz Chambord
    Sour Mix

Grape Crush   Rocks/Shot
    ¾ Oz Chambord
    1 Oz Vodka
    Splash of Sour Mix

Grasshopper   Martini
    1 Oz Green Cream De Menthe
    2 Oz White Cream De Cacao
    Light Cream
    Shaken Well

Great White Sunset   Cocktail
    1.5 Oz Great White Rum
    Pineapple and Orange Juices
    Float of Grenadine
    Garnish With Pineapple Chunks
    and Orange Wheel

Green Tea Cocktail
    1 Oz Irish Whiskey *It's difficult to get this right –*
    ¾ Oz Triple Sec *experiment.*
    ¾ Oz Peach Schnapps
    Lemonade

Grenada
    1.5 Oz Tequila
    Grapefruit Juice
    Splash of Grenadine

H

Hanky Panky Rocks
    1.5 Oz Gin
    1 Oz Sweet Vermouth
    A Dash of Fernet Branca

Harvey Wallbanger Cocktail
    1.5 Oz Vodka
    Orange Juice
    1 Oz Galliano

Head Hunter Cocktail
    1 Oz Bacardi Rum
    1 Oz Captain Morgan Spiced Rum
    Cream De Coconut Mix
    Passion Fruit Juice
    Garnish With Assorted Berries

Heart Break Hill Cocktail
    1.5 Oz Vodka
    1 Oz Pineapple Juice
    ½ Oz Topped With Chambord

Hendricks Style　　　　　　　　Rocks
　　2 Oz Hendricks Gin
　　Rose Petal Syrup
　　And Muddled Cucumber
　　On The Rocks

Here's Looking At You Cosmo　　Martini
　　Deep Eddy Lemon Vodka,　　*Floating Eyeball – made from*
　　Triple Sec, Cranberry Juice a　　*hollowing out a radish and stuffing*
　　Squeeze of Lime and a　　*with a green - pimento olive.*
　　Floating Eyeball　　*scratch peel the side of the radish*
　　　　to give a bloodshot eye effect

Hibiscus Bellini　　　　　　　Champagne Flute
　　Prosecco　　*You can find hibiscus flowers in*
　　House Made Hibiscus Syrup　　*many liquor stores today.*
　　Garnish With Edible Hibiscus Flower

Hibiscus Blackberry Old Fashion　Rocks
　　1.5 Oz Bully Boy Whiskey　　*You should get a specialty ice tray*
　　Soda Water　　*I like spheres, but the trays have*
　　House Made Hibiscus Syrup　　*many different shapes available.*
　　Float Blackberry Brandy
　　Ice Sphere

High Ball　　　　　　　　　Cocktail
　　1.5 Oz Bully Boy Whiskey
　　Ginger Ale
　　Splash of Simple Syrup

　　Honey Ginger Martini　　　　Martini
　　2.5 Oz Reyka Vodka　　*The use of balsamic oil adds a*
　　Newburyport Honey　　*whole new dimension to this*
　　Ginger Balsamic　　*cocktail. Mix it with some simple*
　　Garnish; Orange Wheel　　*syrup – spectacular.*

Honey Dew Margarita | Margarita
Muddled Honey Dew
1.5 Oz Agavalez House Tequila
Splash of Midori
Agave
Strained
Garnish With Honeydew Melon Ball

Honey Hot Toddy | Tea
1.5 Oz Jim Beam Honey Bourbon
Hot Tea
Garnish: Orange Wheel

Hot Cider | Mason Jar
¾ Apple Cider Packet
1.5 Oz Coconut Rum
Sugar Cinnamon Rimmed Glass
Garnish: Cinnamon Stick

Hot Toddy (Table At 10) | Coffee Mug
This Was How We Made It
At My Restaurant. *(Table At 10)*
1.5 Oz Metaxa Brandy
Hot Tea
Honey

This was my grandfather Charlie's cure for the common cold.

Hot Tub | Martini/Rocks
Prosecco
¾ Oz Chambord
1 Oz Vodka
¾ Oz Grand Marnier
Sour Mix
Cranberry Juice
Chilled and Strained

Hot – N- Dirty Martini   Martini
    2.5 Oz Titos Vodka
    Olive and Pepperoncini Juices
    Garnish: Gorgonzola Stuffed
    Pepperoncini

Hugo   Cocktail
    Prosecco
    Sparkling Water
    1.5 Oz St Elderflower
    Splash of Simple Syrup
    Mint Leaf Garnish

Hurricane   Hurricane
    1.5 Oz Rum
    Orange Juice
    Lemonade
    Float of Goslings Black Seal Rum

I

Iceberg Martini   Martini
    2.5 Oz Reyka Vodka   *Similar to the Blue Lagoon*
    Lemonade   *but just a touch of blue curacao*
    A Slight Slash of Blue Curacao   *to give it that ice cold blue tint.*

Icelandic Mule   Cocktail/Beer Glass
    1.5 Oz Reyka Icelandic Vodka
    Ginger Beer
    Splash of Soda Water
    Garnish With a Lime

Indecent Orchid
    1 Oz Vodka
    ½ Oz Chambord
    ½ Oz Peach Schnapps
    Sour Mix
    Grenadine

Cocktail

In Fashion
    1.5 Oz Elijah Craig Bourbon
    ¾ Oz Cointreau
    Black Walnut Bitters

Rocks

Elijah Craig is known as the Father of Bourbon, Cointreau gives this a smooth finish

Island Juice
    1.5 Oz Coconut Rum
    ¾ Oz Midori
    ¾ Oz Banana Liquor
    Pineapple Juice

Hurricane

Italian Flag
    ½ Oz Grenadine
    ½ Oz Melon Liquor
    ½ Oz Rum
    Layered

Pony /Shot

Intense Ginger Martini
    2.5 Oz Nautical Gin
    (With Sea Botanicals)
    Lemonade
    Float ½ Oz of Intense Ginger Liquor

Martini

A bit difficult to get the ingredients for this

(Table At 10) Irish Coffee
    Coffee
    1 Oz West Cork Irish Whiskey
    1 Oz (Kerry Gold) Irish Cream
    Top With Whipped Cream

Coffee Mug

If you can find Kerry Gold – get it ask – some guests don't want Irish cream. West Cork is an underrated whiskey–this was the recipe we used at /table at 10

Irish Gold   Cocktail
    1.5 Oz West Cork Irish Whiskey
    Ginger Ale
    Orange Juice
    ½ Oz Peach Schnapps

Irish Mule   Cocktail
    1.5 Oz Jameson Irish Whiskey   Beer Glass
    Splash of Agave
    Ginger Beer

Irish Shake   Beer Glass
    1.5 Oz Green Cream De Minthe
    Light Cream
    Shaken Frothy
    Topped With Whipped Cream
    A Dash of Gold Dust

J

Jack – O – Lantern   Cocktail
    1.5 Oz Bully Boy Whiskey
    Orange Juice
    Ginger-Ale

Jalapeno Cucumber Margarita   Cocktail
    1.5 Oz Agavalez Tequila
    Muddled Jalapeno and Cucumber
    ¾ Oz Triple Sec
    Sour Mix
    Squeeze Fresh Lime Juice

Jamo and Ginger   Cocktail
    1.5 Oz Jameson Irish Whiskey
    Ginger Ale

Jamaican Me Crazy   Cocktail
    1 Oz Tia Maria
    1 Oz Dark Rum
    Pineapple Juice

Jelly Bean   Shot
    ¾ Oz Sambucca
    ¾ Oz Southern Comfort
    Grenadine

Jenberry Martini   Martini
    2 Oz Tito's Vodka   *Named after our customer Jen, it*
    1 Oz Chambord   *needed a sexy name and story, so I*
    ½ Oz Blue Curacao   *asked a few questions and put it out*
    Cranberry Juice   *on the drink menu.*
    Garnish With Strawberry Slice

One of the bartenders (Jeanne)created a drink for a customer, and they were trying to give it a name. It has to be sexy, and there needs to have a story to it. We came up with a name Jenberry Martini, and now for the story. I asked a few questions: What street do you live on? What type of car do you drive? How do you describe yourself? And this is the story we put on the specials menu:

Jenberry Martini (local) – Indigenous to N Attleborough. This berry is grown in the vineyards of St. Leonard Hope. Known to the native Cherokees as the "Life of the Party."

Jiggle Juice   COCKTAIL
    1.5 Oz Vodka
    ¾ Oz Lillet Blanc
    Sprite,
    Lemonade
    Strawberries and Lime
    Gold Sugar Rimmed Glass

K

Kamikaze   SHOT/ROCKS
- 1 Oz Vodka
- ½ Oz Lime Juice
- ½ Oz Triple Sec

Kentucky Sunrise   COCKTAIL
- 1.5 Oz Bourbon
- Orange Juice
- Grenadine Float

Kentucky Mule   COCKTAIL/BEER
- 1.5 Oz Bourbon
- Ginger Beer
- Splash of Lime Juice

Kentucky Speedball   Copper Glass
- 1.5 Oz Bonded Ry
- ½ Amaro Nonio
- 1 Oz Strawberry Puree
- 1 Oz Lemon Juice
- ½ Oz Balsamic

Kerry Berry   ROCKS
- 1.5 Oz Kerry Gold Irish Liquor
- 1 Oz Chambord
- Splash of Light Cream

Key Lime Pie Martini   MARTINI
- 2 Oz Blu Chair Key Lime Pie Rum
- 1 Oz Lime Rum
- Lime Juice
- Graham Cracker Rimmed Glass

Kioki Coffee

    1oz House Brandy

    ¾ Oz Kahlua

    ¾ Oz Dark Cream De Cocoa

    Topped With Whipped Cream And

    Mini Chocolate Chips

COFFE MUG

From the "way back machine" but still one of my favorites.

Kir Royale

    1.5 Oz Cream De Casis *(Chambord)*

    Topped With Prosecco

CHAMPAGNE FLUTE

Kool Aid

    1.5 Oz Vodka

    1 Oz Melon Liquor

    Splash ½ Oz of Amaretto

    Cranberry Juice

ROCKS

Kukoo Kunuku Cocktail

    1.5 Oz Coconut Rum

    1 Oz Melon Liquor

    Pineapple Juice

COCKTAIL

You know it if you have been to Aruba!

Lemon Balm Cocktail

Lemondrop Martini

L

Lemon Balm

    1.5 Oz Malfy Italian Gin

    Lemonade

    Muddled Lemon Balm

    Garnish With Lemon Wheel

COCKTAIL

Malfy is imported from Italy it is a great lemon flavored gin this is a great introduction exposure to gin

Lemon Basil Martini

    Muddled Basil Leaves

    2.5 Oz Citrus (Lemon) Vodka

    Splash of Lemonade

    Dash of Simple Syrup

    STRAINED

    Garnish With Lemon Wheel and Basil

MARTINI

Lemon Crush

    1 Oz Lemoncello

    1 Oz Cytron Vodka

    Splash of Triple Sec

    Splash of Lemonade

    Fresh Squeezed Lemon Juice

COCKTAIL

Lemon Drop Martini
    Fresh Squeezed Lemon
    2.5 Oz Cytron Vodka
    Splash of Limoncello
    Splash of Lemonade
    Garnish With Sugar Rim and Lemon

MARTINI

Lemon Meringue/Pie Martini
    2 Oz Stoli Vanilla Vodka
    1 Oz Limoncello
    Splash of Light Cream
    Splash of Soda Water
    SHAKE WELL
    Graham Cracker Rimmed Glass

MARTINI
Some recipes call for egg white – gives a nice foam on top – I tend to recommend staying away from using egg whites unless you know what you're doing.

Lemonade (Pink)
    1 Oz Rum
    1 Oz Citrus Vodka
    Ginger-Ale
    1.2 Oz Triple Sec
    Sour Mix
    Dash of Grenadine

COCKTAIL

Let's Get Kinky
    1.5 Oz Kinky (Pink) Vodka
    Blood Orange Mixer
    Splash of Sprite
    Garnish With an Orange Slice

HURRICANE
Sometimes you need to use your imagination!

Lisa Beer
    Any Beer
    Over Ice In a Wine Glass

WINE GLASS
Lisa was a customer who had it her way.

Love Potion #9
   1 Oz Vodka
   1 Oz Amaretto
   1 Oz Peach Schnapps
   Grenadine

MARTINI/COCKTAIL

For any Love Potion cocktail, the use of dry ice can change the entire complexion of this cocktail – so cool. Careful handling dry ice. use a tea strainer and get the smoke effect.

Love Potion
   2 Oz Raspberry Vodka
   Pineapple Juice
   1 Oz Chambord

MARTINI

Love Potion (Asian Inspired)
   1 Oz Bacardi Rum
   1 Oz Banana Liquor
   ¾ Oz Orange Curacao/ Or Triple Sec
   Pineapple Juice Passion Fruit Juice

COCKTAIL

Mimosa

Christmas Cocktail

Mojito

M

Macaroon

    1 Oz Coconut Rum

    1 Oz Amaretto

    ½ Oz White Creme De Cacao

    Splash of Light Cream

    Garnish With Coconut Flakes

MARTINI

The cookie never tasted this good!

Macintosh Martini MARTINI
    2 Oz Apple Pucker
    ½ Oz Cinnamon Schnapps
    Pineapple Juice
    Splash of Sour Mix

Madras COCKTAIL
    1.5 Oz Vodka
    Cranberry Juice
    Orange Juice

Mambo Punch COCKTAIL / BEER MUG
    1.5 Oz Vodka
    Pineapple and Orange Juices
    Simple Syrup
    Splash of St Elders
    Top With Ginger Beer

Mango Martini MARTINI
    1.5 Oz Mandarin Vodka
    1 Oz Raspberry Vodka
    Orange Juice

Margarita MARGARITA
    1.5 Oz Tequila
    ¾ Oz Triple Sec
    Lime Juice
    Sour Mix
    Splash of OJ
    Salted Rim
    Garnish With a Lime

Mai Tai

- 1 Oz Don Q White Rum
- ½ Oz Triple Sec
- ½ Oz Amaretto OR Orgeat
- Orange Bitters
- Passion Juice
- Float ½ Oz of Goslings Black Seal Rum

HURRICANE

It gets close to the taste from a Chinese restaurant. You may want to add just a dash of apricot brandy.

Mandrin Martini

- 2.5 Oz Absolute Mandrin
- Cranberry Juice
- Sugar Rimmed Glass

MARTINI

Mango Martini

- 2 Oz Vodka
- Mango Puree
- ¾ Oz Triple Sec
- Splash of OJ
- Garnish With Mango Chunks

MARTINI

Manhattan

- 2.5 Oz Bully Boy Whiskey
- ¾ Oz Sweet Vermouth
- Garnish With a Cherry

MARTINI

Any whiskey will do – I like using a locally distilled brand like Bully Boy from Boston.

Maple Walnut Old Fashion

- 1.5 Oz Maple Bourbon Or Whiskey
- Soda Water
- Black Walnut Bitters
- Garnish With Bacon Strip

ROCKS

Any bourbon with a tablespoon of maple syrup. The Black Walnut Bitters adds a great flavor profile

Maple Walnut Breeze

PINT GLASS

 1.5 Oz Hazlenut Liquor
 ¾ Oz Amaretto Dolce
 Ice Cream Mix
 Topped With Whipped Cream
 Maple Syrup Drizzle

Martini

MARTINI

Sometimes the original satisfies
– stirred, not shaken

 2.5 Oz Gin Or Vodka
 ¾ Oz Dry Vermouth
 Olives Or Lemon Twist

Melon Ball Cocktail

COCKTAIL

You'll be ready for summer with
some of these!

 1 Oz Vodka
 1 Oz Midori – Melon Liquor
 Pineapple and Orange Juices
 Garnish With Pineapple Chunks And a Cherry

Merry Mimosa

CHAMPAGNE FLUTE

A pretty drink for christmas

 Prosecco
 1.5 Oz Pama Pomegranate Liquor
 Splash of Cranberry Juice
 Red Sugar Rimmed Glass
 Garnish With Thyme and Cranberries

Midnight Marauder

MARTINI

A favorite contributed by Vuolo's
Restaurant

 2.5 Oz Bourbon
 ¾ Oz Demerara Syrup
 2 Dash of Orange Bitters
 4 Dashes of Chocolate Bitters

Mind Eraser

COCKTAIL

The straw is important; pour the
Kahlua in first, add the vodka gently
next and top off with soda water

 Layered
 1 Oz Kahlua
 1 Oz Vodka
 Fill With Soda Water
 Drink Through a Straw

Mint Julep
  1.5 Oz Elijah Craig Bourbon
  Muddled Mint Leaves
  Soda Water
  Splash of Simple Syrup

COCKTAIL
An official cocktail of the
Kentucky Derby

Mistletoe Margarita
  1.5 Oz Tequila
  ¾ Oz Triple Sec
  ½ Oz Simple Syrup
  Cranberry Juice
  Squeeze of Lime
  Sugar Rimmed Glass
  Float Cranberries On Top

MARGARITA

Mojito
  1.5 Oz Coconut Rum
  Soda Water
  Raw Sugar
  Muddled Mint Leaves
  Garnish: Mint

ROCKS

Moscow Mule
  1.5 Oz Vodka
  Ginger Beer
  Over Ice
  Garnish With a Lime

CUP / PINT
Any spirit with ginger beer is a
mule-try to get a copper cup it helps
to keep the temperature of the drink.

Mounds Bar
  1.5 Oz Coconut Rum
  ¾ Oz Dark Cream De Cocoa
  Splash of Light Cream
  Garnish With Coconut Rim Glass

ROCKS

Mudslide
FROZEN/SHAKE

1 Oz Kahlua
1 Oz Vodka
1 Oz Baileys
Splash of Dark Cream De Cocao
 Or Dorda Chocolate Liquor
Ice Cream
Line Glass With Hershey's Syrup
Top With Whipped Cream

*Makes a great martini – not frozen
substitute light cream for ice cream.*

N

Naked On The Beach
COCKTAIL:

1.5 Oz Peach Schnapps
Cranberry Juice

Nervous Breakdown
ROCKS

(Also Known As Suffering Bastard)
1.5 Oz Vodka
Top With Chambord
And Soda Water

New Fashion
ROCKS

1.5 Oz Elijah Craig Bourbon
¾ Oz Amaretto
Simple Syrup
Orange Bitters

Nigrone
MARTINI

1 Oz Gin
1 Oz Sweet Vermouth
1 Oz Campari

Nigrone Update   ROCKS/MARTINI
    1 Oz Handricks Gin
    1 Oz Aperol
    1 Oz Lilett Blanc

Not Your Mother's Iced Coffee   ROCKS
    Iced Coffee
    1.5 Oz Cape Cod Coffee Vodka
    1 Oz Rum Chata

Nuts and Berries   ROCKS
    1.5 Oz Frangelico
    1.5 Oz Chambord
    Splash of Light Cream

Nutcracker   ROCKS
    1 Oz Vanilla Vodka
    1 Oz Frangelico *(Hazelnut Liquor)*
    ¾ Oz Amaretto
    Top off With Light Cream

Nutty Irishman   ROCKS
    1.5 Oz Baileys Irish Cream (Kerry Gold)
    1.5 Oz Frangelico *(Hazelnut Liquor)*

Oatmeal Cookie   SHOT/COCKTAIL
    1 Oz Baileys Irish Cream
    ½ Oz Cinnamon Schnapps
     Splash ½ Oz of Kalhua
    Top With Light Cream

Old Cuban   COCKTAIL
1.5 Oz Rum (*Usually Dark*)
Lime Juice
Simple Syrup
Bitters
Mint Leaves
Sparkling Wine
Garnish With Mint Leaves

Orange Blossom   COCKTAIL
1.5 Oz Sky Blood Orange Vodka
Pineapple and Cranberry Juices

Orgasm   ROCKS
½ Vodka
½ Kalhua
½ Amaretto
½ Triple Sec
½ Baileys
Top With Light Cream
Served Chilled and Strained

Oreo Cookie   FROZEN
1 Oz Vanilla Vodka
1 Oz Baileys
Dash of Creme De Minthe
1 Oz Dark Crème De Cacao
Vanilla Ice Cream
Garnish With Oreo Cookies
Or Crushed Oreo Cookie Rimmed Glass

Keep Up With the Trends

Trends come and go – and then they return! Cocktails like an Old Fashioned comes back in style every 7 years or so. Retro drinks from the 80s and 90s make comebacks, the roaring 20s and the Speakeasy find their way to the top over and over. But more than the drinks, it's the creativity. It's the use of herbs, oils, smoke, etc. Bar tools like beakers or eyedroppers, bar torch, lemon press, egg whites, home-made whipped cream, infused spirits, all of these are part of the show.

Old Fashioned
  2 Oz Bully Boy Whiskey
  Raw Sugar Pack
  Soda Water
  A Few Dashes of Bitters
  Lightly Muddled Orange and Cherry

Rocks
*This classic makes a comeback
every few years*

Oreo Cookie Shake Up

Peeps Martini

Pistachio Muffin Martini

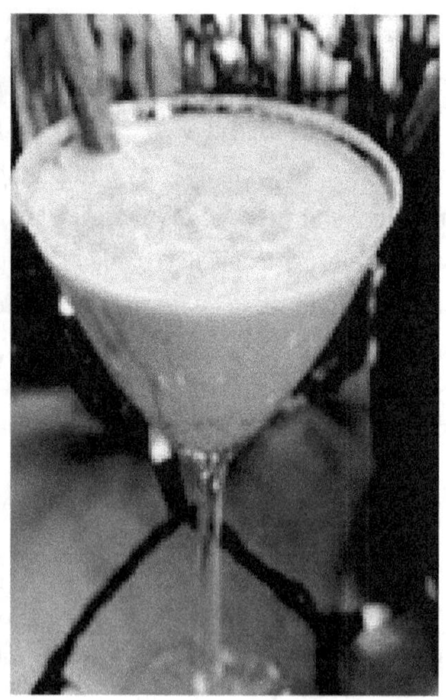

Pumpkin Pie Martini

P

Pain Killer

    1.5 Don Q White Rum
    Pineapple Juice
    Cream De Coconut
    Shaken and Served Over Ice
    Garnish With Pineapple Chunks
    Add Nutmeg (Ask About Allergies)

Rocks

Be careful using nutmeg due to allergies. Always ask the customer about allergies.

Palm Breeze

    1.5 Oz Don Q White Rum
    Pineapple Juice
    Splash of Cranberry Juice

Cocktail

Paloma (Pink)   Cocktail Glass
    1.5 Oz Tequila   *Even I can drink tequila like this.*
    (*¾ Oz Pama Pomegranate*)
    Soda Water
    Simple Syrup
    Pinch of Salt
    Grapefruit Juice
    Garnish With Lime

Pancakes and Syrup   Footed Shot Glass
    1 Oz Jameson Irish Whiskey   *Breakfast in a glass! The after flavor*
    1 Oz Butterscotch Schnapps   *is remarkable. Perfect for brunch.*
    No Ice
    Chase With Shot of Orange Juice
    Garnish With Strip of Bacon

Paradiso   Rocks
    1.5 Oz Orange Vodka
    ½ Oz Limoncello
    ½ Oz Aperol
    Fresh Squeezed Orange

Palm Breeze   Cocktail
    1.5 Oz Rum
    Pineapple Juice
    Orange Juice

Peanut Butter and Jelly   Footed Shot Glass
    1.5 Oz Frangelico (*Hazelnut Liquor*) *Just like your mom made on fresh*
    ¾ Oz Chambord   *Wonder white bread.*
    No Ice

Peanut-Butter Cup Martini   Martini
    2 Oz Peanut Butter Whiskey,
    1 Oz Dark Cream De Cacao
    ½ Oz Irish Cream, With Whipped Cream
    And a Reese's Cup

Peanut Butter Cup Shake-Up   Shaker Glass
    1.5 Oz Peanut Butter Whiskey
    Light Cream
    1 Oz Dark Cream De Cacao
    Shaken and Served Over Ice
    Garnished With Crushed Reese's Pieces

Peach Bellini   Champagne Flute
    Prosecco
    House Made Peach Puree
Pear Bellini   Champagne Flute
    Prosecco
    Float of Pear Vodka

Pearl Harbor   Cocktail
    1 Oz Vodka
    1 Oz Midori (Melon Liquor)
    Pineapple Juice
    Garnish With Orange and Cherry

Peeps Martini   Martini
    2.5 Oz Whipped Cream Vodka   *Be careful – the Peeps tend to melt!*
    Or Stoli Vanilla
    Garnish With a Peep

Peppermint Patti   Cocktail
    ¾ Oz Peppermint Schnapps
    1.5 Oz Dark Cream De Cocoa

Pickle Back   Neat/Rocks
    1.5 Oz Jameson Whiskey
    Side of Dill Pickle Juice
    Garnish With a Pickle Chip

Piece of Ass   Cocktail
    1.5 Oz Southern Comfort   *Made especially for Donnette as a*
    1 Oz Amaretto   *substitute for an Alabama Slammer*
    Sour Mix

Pina Colada   Pint Beer Glass
    1.5 Oz Coconut Rum
    Pineapple Juice
    Pina Colada Mix
    Whipped Cream
    Garnish With Pineapple Chunks

Pink Squirrel   Martini
    1 Oz Crem D' Noyaux (Almond)
    1.5 Oz White Creme De Cacao
    Light Cream
    Add Grenadine For Color

Pineapple-Mango & Basil Sangria   Wine Glass
    White Wine
    Passion Juice
    Splash of Sprite
    1 Oz St Elders
    Garnish With Basil Leaf and Mango Chunks

Pineapple Margarita   Margarita
    1.5 Oz Casamigos Tequila,
    1 Oz Triple Sec,
    Pineapple Juice, and Orange Juice,
    Squeeze of Fresh Lime,
    Garnished With an Orange Wheel and Pineapple Chunk

Pineapple Upside Down Cake Martini — Martini

2 Oz Stoli Vanilla Vodka
Pineapple Juice
Drops of Grenadine

The grenadine should drop to the bottom of the glass – if you mix all the ingredients it is also known as a cherry cheesecake

Pistachio Muffin Martini — Martini

2 Oz Irish Cream
1 Oz Amaretto Dolce
Splash of Light Cream
Blue Curacao (Just a Dash For Color)
Graham Cracker Rimmed Glass

It's like being at the bakery.

(Vuolo's) Pistachio Martini — Martini

1.5 Oz Pistachio Cream Liquor
¾ Oz Vanilla Vodka
¾ Oz Irish Cream Liquor
¾ Oz Amaretto
House -Made Pistachio Cream

Planter's Punch — Cocktail

1 Oz Rum
1 Oz Dark Rum
Grenadine
Oj
Sour Mix

Plum Bellini — Champagne Flute

Prosecco
House Made Plumb Puree

PMS — Shot

½ Oz Peach Schnapps
½ Oz Malibu Coconut Rum
½ Oz Stoli Vanilla Vodka

Pomegranate Martini   Martini
    2.5 Oz Parma Pomegranate Liquor
    ¾ Oz Triple Sec
    Cranberry Juice

Pumpkin Pie Martini   Martini
    2 Oz Fultons Pumpkin   *This is comfort in a glass. better*
    Cream Liquor   *than the pie ! have some fun –*
    1 Oz Stoli Vanilla Vodka   *Add a dollop of whipped cream*
    Graham Cracker Rimmed Glass   *and sprinkle graham cracker crumbs*
                                        on top for looks

Q

Qualud   Shot
    ¾ Oz B&B
    ¾ Oz Grand Marnier

R

Raspberry-Lemonade Margarita   Margarita
    1.5 Oz Tequila (House)
    Raspberry Puree
    Lemonade
    Lime Juice
    Garnish With Raspberries

Red Death   Shot
    ½ Oz Amaretto   *A favorite at Three Cheers*
    ½ Oz Sloe Gin
    ½ Oz Southern Comfort
    ½ Oz Vodka
    ½ Oz Triple Sec
    Orange Juice

Red Eye
    Tomato Juice
    Beer
    (supposed to be good for hangover)

Beer Mug
Not sure if it was a hangover cure – but the guys say it helps the day after a drinking binge.

Red Pear Martini
    1 Oz Coconut Rum
    1 Oz Apple Pucker
    1 Oz Pear Vodka Or Syrup
    Cranberry Juice

Martini
Coconut Rum and Apple Pucker = Pear Taste I make my own pear vodka - soak the pears in a jar of vodka, looks great and customers love it.

Riviera Cocktail
    1.5 Oz Hennessey Cognac
    Prosecco
    Splash of Apple Cider
    Over Ice

Wine Glass

Rob Roy
    2 Oz Scotch
    3/4 Oz Sweet Vermouth

Martini

Root Beer Float
    1.5 Oz Rum Chata
    Root Beer
    Over Ice With a Scoop
    of Vanilla Ice Cream

Mason Jar
Just like your grandma made – well a little!

Root Beer – California
    1 Oz Vodka
    1 Oz Kahlua
    Coke and Soda Water
    Top With Galliano
    Splash of Root Beer

Cocktail
It helps if you add root beer

Rose' Cocktail — Wine Glass
- Rose' Wine
- Soda Water
- Splash of Balsamic Grapefruit
- Splash of Simple Syrup
- Garnish With Orange and Cherry
- Over Ice

Rose' Collins — Cocktail
- 1.5 Oz Gin
- Lillet Blanc Or Rose'
- Lime Juice
- Grapefruit Soda
- Garnish With Grapefruit Slice

Rose' Spritzer — Wine Glass
- Rose' Wine
- Ginger Ale
- Splash of Simple Syrup
- Over Ice
- Sugar Rimmed Glass

Roy Rogers Gone Rogue — Cocktail
- 1.5 Oz Cherry Vodka
- Coke
- Grenadine

Younger patrons (under 50) may not know Roy Rogers – this was a drink for boys and Shirley Temple was for girls.

Rum Runner — Cocktail
- 1 Oz Light Rum
- 1 Oz Dark Rum
- Pineapple Juice
- Oj
- Cranberry Juice
- Top With Sprite

Run By The Charles
   2.5 Oz Gin
   Just a Drop of Dry Vermouth
   1 Oz Dirty Olive Juice
   Garnish With Gorgonzola Stuffed Olive

Martini
   Preferably Bully Boy Gin
   "Love That Dirty Water"

Rusty Nail
   1 Oz Scotch
   1 Oz Drambui

Snifter

Reeses Shake Up

Sunny – Tini

Watermelon Martini

S

Salted Caramel Pretzel   Rocks
    1 Oz Stoli Vanilla Vodka   *Dorda is rich and creamy*
    1 Oz Dorda Salted Caramel Liquor
    Caramel Sauce Rimmed Glass
    Crushed Pretzel Rimmed Glass

Salted Caramel White Russian   Rocks
    1 Oz Vodka
    1 Oz Dorda Salted Caramel Liquor
    Splash of Kahlua
    Top With Splash of Light Cream
    Rimmed Glass of Caramel Sauce and Sea Salt

Salty Dog   Cocktail
    1.5 Oz Vodka
    Grapefruit Juice
    Salted Rim

Sangria — Wine / Hurricane

Red Or White Wine
1 Oz Peach Schnapps
¾ Oz Triple Sec
Sprite
Top With Orange Juice

Add Some cut up fruit and it's a homerun. Keep it simple and make it on demand. No need to make a big batch

Satins Whiskers — Cocktail

1.5 Oz Orange Vodka
¾ Oz Triple Sec
Orange Juice
2 Dashes of Orange Bitters

Scarlet O'hara — Cocktail

1.5 Oz Southern Comfort
Cranberry Juice
Sour Mix
Garnish With a Cherry

Scrambler Cocktail — Cocktail

1.5 Oz House Tequila
Orange Juice
Float ¼ Oz of Blackberry Brandy

Screaming Viking — Cocktail

1.5 Oz Coconut Rum
Cranberry and Pineapple Juice
Float ½ Oz of Goslings Black Seal Rum
Garnish: Cucumber Slice

Made Famous From The Tv Series Cheers And We Sold a Lot of Them At Faneuil Hall – Boston

Scroppino (Venetian) — Martini

2 Oz Lemon Vodka
Prosecco
Whisked Or Shaken Frothy
1 Scoop of Lemon Sorbet

Sea Breeze   Cocktail
    1.5 Oz Vodka
    Grapefruit Juice
    Cranberry Juice

Sex On The Beach   Cocktail
    1.5 Oz Vodka
    ½ Oz Peach Schnapps
    Orange Juice
    Cranberry Juice

Side Car   Cocktail
    1.5 Oz Brandy
    ½ Oz Triple Sec
    Sour Mix

Singapore Sling   Cocktail
    1.5 Oz House Gin
    Sour Mix and Soda Water
    Top With ½ Oz Cherry Brandy
    Or Grenadine

Slippery Nipple   Shot/Pony
    1 Oz Sambucca   *After you float the Baileys, take up a*
    Float ½ Oz Baileys   *drop an eye drop of grenadine, hold*
    Drop of Grenadine   *above the glass and release – the*
                                          effect looks like a nipple

Slow Gin Fizz   Cocktail
    1.5 Oz Sloe Gin
    Sour Mix
    Soda Water

Smoked Chili Margarita
  1.5 Oz Tequila
  Agave Nectar
  ¾ Oz Triple Sec
  Orange Juice
  Garnished With Grilled Chili Peppers

Margarita
This would be a great drink to infuse with smoke.

Keep Up With the Trends 2

Making infused spirits is not that difficult. I like to make pear infused vodka. Vodka is very adaptable to the taste of what its infused with) In a large jar add vodka, then peel several pears and let them soak in the vodka for a few days. I sometimes cheat and add some pear vodka. To make a Stoli-Doli - The same process can be done with Stoli vanilla vodka and fresh pineapples ring. This was a popular 1990s shot, and the jars of soaking fruit look really cool on the bar.

Smores Campfire Martini
  2 Oz Stoli Vanilla or Marshmallow Vodka
  1.Oz Dark Cream De Cocoa
  Splash of Light Cream
  Graham Cracker Rimmed Glass
  Toasted Marshmallow

Martini
Use a torch lighter to set the marshmallow on fire – let the scent fill the bar area put it out by rolling it on top of the alcohol camping has never been better.

Snickers Bar
  (Also Known As a Sit On My Face)
  1 Oz Kahlua
  1 Oz Fratella Hazelnut Liquor
  1 Oz Irish Cream
  Served On The Rocks

Rocks
Not sure how this name came about from the 1980s.

Snow Flake Martini   Martini
    2 Oz Don Q Coconut Rum
    1 Oz Rum Chata
    Splash of ½ Oz Whipped Cream Vodka
    Or Vanilla Vodka
    Coconut Flaked Rimmed Glass

Sombrero   Cocktail
    1.5 Oz. Kahlua
    Light Cream

Southern Comfort Manhattan   Martini
    2.5 Oz Southern Comfort
    1 Oz Sweet Vermouth
    Garnished With a Cherry

Spring Fling   Martini
    1.5 Titos Vodka
    ½ Oz St Elders
    Prosecco
    Splash of Orange Juice

Spagliato Milano   Cocktail
    Sparkling Wine
    ¾ Oz Campari
    ¾ Oz Sweet Vermouth

Sparkling Spring Martini   Martini
    2 Oz Pear Vodka
    ½ Oz St Elder
    Simple Syrup
    Topped With Lemonade
    Garnish: Cucumber and Mint

Spicy Mint Avocado Margarita   Margarita
Muddled: Avocado, Mint, Jalapenos
1.5 Oz Tequila
¾ Oz Triple Sec
Lime Juice
Splash of Sour Mix
Best To Strain This Into The Glass
Garnish With Mint and Jalapenos

Spicy Spicy Scary Mary   Pint Glass
1.5 Oz Vodka   *It's hot – be sure to warn guests!*
Bloody Mary Mix
¼ Tea Spoon of Horseradish
Dash of Bitters
Couple Dashes of Habanero Pepper Sauce
And a Squeeze of Jalapeno Puree
Garnish With a Green Olive

Strawberry Bubbly   Champagne Flute
Prosecco   *Strawberries and simple syrup*
House Made Strawberry Puree   *blended*
Garnish With a Strawberry

Strawberry Shortcake   Pint Beer Glass
1.5 Oz Cream De Banana
Splash of ½ Oz House Amaretto
Strawberry Mix
Splash of Light Cream
Top With Whipped Cream
Garnish With Slice of Strawberry

Strawberry Banana Boat Shake   Hurricane
1.5 Oz Vanilla Vodka
Strawberry and Banana Mix
Splash of Pineapple Juice
Shaken Frothy

Seelbach Martini

    2 Oz Elijah Craig Bourbon
    ½ Oz Triple Sec
    Dash of Orange Bitters
    Topped With Prosecco
    Garnish With an Orange Peel

Martini

There are a few stories to contribute about this – it was named after the famed Louisiana hotel and was mixed by mistake? years later, the recipe was stumbled upon.

Stelatini

    2 Oz Stoli Vanilla Vodka
    1 Oz Amaretto
    1 Oz White Cream De Cocoa
    Pineapple and Cranberry Juices
    Shake Well

Martini

Named for our restaurant: Stella Osteria

Stinger

    1.5 Oz Brandy
    1 Oz White Creme De Menthe
    Shaken and Strained Over Ice

Rocks

Surfer On Acid

    ¾ Oz Jägermeister
    ¾ Coconut Rum
    Pineapple Juice

Shot / Rocks

Sugar Cookie Martini

    2 Oz Burnetts Sugar Cookie Vodka
    Splash of ½ Oz Kahlua
    Splash of Cream
    Sugar Cookie Rimmed Glass

Martini

Sunny-Tini

    2 Oz Orange Vodka
    1 Oz Triple Sec
    Orange Juice
    Garnish With Sugar Rim and Orange Wheel

Martini

Sweet Nutz
    1.5 Oz Vanilla Vodka
    ¾ Oz Hazelnut Liquor
    ¾ Oz Caramel Vodka
    Topped With Whipped Cream
    And Chocolate Treats

Rocks
Add a little sweetness to your life

T

Tequila Sunrise
    1.5 Oz House Tequila
    Orange Juice
    A <u>Float</u> of Grenadine
    Garnish With an Orange

Cocktail
Definitely not a drink to shake or stir. Why? It needs to look like a sunrise.

Tiki Bubbles
    1.5 Oz Coconut Rum
    Prosecco
    Pineapple Juice

Cocktail
My friend Paula was missing the Caribbean so we came up with this cocktail, and by coincidence – we had the steel drums music

Tickle My Coconutz
    1.5 Oz Don Q Coconut Rum,
    1 Oz Dark Cream De Caoca,
    Splash ½ Oz of Dorda Chocolate Liquor
    Coconut Flake Rimmed Glass.

Martini

Toasted Almond
    1.5 Oz Amaretto
    1 Oz Kahlua
    Light Cream

Cocktail
Make it a Roasted Toasted Almond by adding 1 oz of vodka

Tie Me To The Bedposts — Cocktail

Make life exciting!

- 1 Oz Vodka
- 1 Oz Elijah Craig Small Batch Bourbon
- ½ Oz Amaretto
- Orange Juice
- Grenadine
- Garnish With Orange Wheel

Tiramisu Martini — Martini

- 2 Oz Vanilla Vodka
- ¾ Oz House Amaretto
- ¾ Oz Kahlua
- Splash of Light Cream
- Sprinkle Some Cocoa Powder

Tom Collins — Cocktail / Collins

- 1.5 Oz Gin
- Sour Mix
- Soda Water
- Garnish With Lemon Wheel

Tootsie Roll — Rocks

- 1.5 Oz Dark Creme De Cacao
- Orange Juice

Torino — Rocks

- 1 Oz Aperol
- ¾ Oz Dry Vermouth
- ¾ Oz Triple Sec
- Muddled Orange

Triple O's
    1.5 Oz Orange Vodka
    ¾ Oz Triple Sec
    Splash of Orange Juice
    Garnish With Fresh
    Squeezed Orange

Martini

This was an adaptation from the 007 drink. It came to light the week that Whitey Bulger was arrested. We added an extra "O" and named it Triple O's after his hangout Bar on Broadway– South Boston

U

Universal Martini
    Oz Gin
    ¾ Oz Dry Vermouth
    ¾ Oz Port Wine
    Dash of Bitters
    Garnish With Lemon Peel Twist

Martini

Universal
    ¾ Oz Mellon Liquor (Midori)
    ¾ Oz Grapefruit Juice
    ¾ Ox Vodka
    Layered
    Garnish With Grapefruit Slice

Shot

V

Vampire's Kiss
    Prosecco
    1 Oz Chambord

Champagne Flute

Shake Vs Stir

I am more of a stir mixologist. If you are going to shake – do it with flair. and make the pour out of the shaker and into the glass be dramatic. Both shaking and stirring have their place, use them appropriately. Don't "bruise the alcohol" unnecessarily. and please don't shake a tequila sunrise!

James Bond started this whole thing by ordering his martini shaken, not stirred!

Vanilla – Cinnamon Coke Cocktail
> 1.5 Oz Stoli Vanilla Vodka and Coke,
> House Made Cinnamon Syrup

Vesper Martini Martini
> 1.5 Oz Vodka
> 1 Oz Gin
> 1 Oz Lillet Blanc
> Lemon Twist Garnish

First appeared in 1953 Casino Royale movie, named after James Bond 's love interest and fictional double agent Vesper Lynd.

Vito Collins Cocktail
> 1.5 Oz Gin
> 1 Oz Limoncello
> Soda Water

Vodka Gimlet Rocks
> 1.5 Oz Vodka
> ¾ Oz Lime Juice
> Garnish With a Lime of Course

W

Ward Eight — Rocks
1.5 Oz Bully Boy Whiskey
Shaken With Orange and Lemon
Juices
Served Over Ice

*Reportedly created in Boston 1898
after a politician who represented
and was the "boss" of the city's
Eighth Ward (along the Charles River)*

Washington Apple — Martini
1.5 Oz Crown Royal
1 Oz Apple Pucker
Cranberry Juice

Simple and delicious

Watermelon — Cocktail
1.5 Oz Vodka
3/4 Oz Midori
Cranberry Juice

White Russian — Cocktail
1 Oz Vodka
1 Oz Kahlua
Light Cream

Woo Woo — Shot
1 Oz Vodka
3/4 Oz Peach Schnapps
Cranberry Juice

X

Xaviera — Rocks
1 Oz Kahlua
1 Oz Amaretto
1/2 Oz Triple Sec

Y

Yankee Prince
Oz Gin
¾ Oz Grand Marnier
Orange Juice
Garnish With Filbert Nut

Z

Zombie   Cocktail
1 Oz Bacardi Rum
1 Oz Myers Dark Rum
½ Oz Triple Sec
Orange Juice
Sour Mix
Splash of Grenadine

Miscellaneous Cocktails

Story 2: ***WORKING THE HOLIDAYS***

I do like to spend the holidays with my family, I guess I'm a traditionalist. But just the big holidays like Thanksgiving, Christmas Eve and day. Don't get me wrong I have worked my share of holiday shifts, especially if the other staff has children, I would work to give them the night off. Of course when I worked the bar it was not as popular as it is today to go out to a restaurant on the holidays. That's a game changer, because today you can make some good money on those shifts.

The bar customers always seem to make it in for a cocktail before they went off to be with their families. On Thanksgiving and New Year's Day there is usually a football pool to make it a bit more exciting. Neighborhood places always seemed to have a big complimentary bowl of eggnog. It started out creamy, and as the day went on, and when the owner wasn't looking, somehow extra brandy fell into the bowl.

Of course holidays always brought in the most tips. I was lucky, regular customers usually gave me an envelope to thank me for the service I gave all year., a nice gesture, no matter how much it was.

There was always those customers who just plain "irked me." Like the guy who came in at 4 p.m. on Christmas Eve, when he knew we were closing at 4:30. He started to order a meal and said his brother was meeting him. Then he wanted to play 20 games of keno, it takes easily over an hour to get through that many games. The place being empty wasn't enough of a hint for him. Hate to be the Grinch, but I had to remind him that the doors were closing at 4:30, meaning everyone had to be out.

Another gem was on New Year's Eve. We planned to close at 9 p.m., enough time for people to come out to dinner and get to whatever party they were going to before midnight. Two couples walked in about 8 p.m., we informed them we were closing early, but there was enough time for dinner, knowing they probably weren't going to be out of there before 10 p.m. Usually two hours is enough time for dinner. First it was dinner, then deserts, now they are on the second round of after dinner drinks and it's 10 p.m.. They were having a good time and seemed like decent people. However, they didn't recognize that they were the only ones in the place. I hate to be the "common sense police" but at 10:30 when they wanted to order another round, I had to inform them that they would have to order the next round somewhere else!

LESSON LEARNED: Staff members have lives too. Always let the customer know up front what the limits are. It makes it easier when you have to explain closing time.

COFFEE DRINKS

All topped with whipped cream unless requested not. It's nice if you can top these off with cocoa powder, various colored sugars, and/or gold and silver dusts

Dutch	Vandermint
French	Grand Marnier
Irish	Irish Whiskey and Baileys (if asked for)
Jamaican	Tia Maria
Spanish	Brandy And Kahlua Laced With Grand Marnier
Roman	Galliano
Kioki	Brandy, Kahlua, and Dark Creme De Cacao
Caribbean	Rum and Kahlua
Coffee Royale	Brandy
Chateau	Kahlua and Baileys
Mediterranean	Kahlua, White Creme De Cacao Whipped Cream and Pour a Splash of Frangelico Over
Nutty Irishman	Frangelico and Baileys
Hot Toddy	Hot Water, Whiskey, Sugar – No Coffee
Winta – Time Hot Toddy	Metaxa Brandy, Hot Tea, and Honey (Medicinal)
No Name	Rum Chata and Coffee
Pumpkin Spice	Fulton's Harvest Pumpkin Pie Cream Liquor

SHORTS – *Summer Work ... But Worth a Mention*

A)

I was an alternative high school teacher for a number of years. Every summer, in addition to my regular bar job, I would look for extra work as a bartender. During my lunch hour one day, I took a ride to Revere Beach. I noticed a place was looking for help, so I went to the door and knocked. This small but vibrant woman with the biggest smile in the world opened the door. I asked if they were looking for bartenders and she said yes. "Can I apply?" I asked.

She said, "Sure, can you start now?" I looked at her stunned. I didn't want to miss the chance to get a summer job. "I'm on lunch, but I can come back tonight."

"OK great, I'll see you at 4 p.m.," she said. This should have been a red flag!

She met me at 4, gave me a quick five minute instruction on prices, glassware, and the glass washer and then said – "Don't take any shit from anyone, I have to run out. I'll be back to close." Next up was her boyfriend, his car broke down and he asked to borrow my car (another red flag) As it turned out, this place was a "bucket of blood." The inmates (customers) ran the asylum, that is unless the warden was there – and she wasn't always there. I was jumping over the bar nightly to break up fights, chase down customers walking out with beers, regulars wanted the music overbearingly loud, which kept normal people away. But Angie liked me, always paid me, and let me get away with a lot of stuff. I'm glad I met her during my life, she was 'good people' and I actually learned a lot from her. She had a lot of 'wise guy' friends and she always made sure they tipped me well. I was never able to figure out why she owned a place like that.

LESSON LEARNED: Think before jumping in.

B)

Another summer I got my first "real" bartending job at a nice Revere Beach Restaurant. This place was busy during the summer. By real bar job, I mean this place wasn't just beers and shots, I had to actually make cocktails, frozen drinks, and serve food too. I was excited to learn until the person who was supposed to train me didn't show up. I was on my own, yikes, talk about being in the weeds! A 200 seat restaurant, a 15 seat bar, and I was responsible for the raw bar (shrimp, oysters, and cherrystones). Not to mention I had to look up all the drinks that were being ordered (Sex on the Beach, Pearl Harbor, etc.) They had an island oasis machine, I went to make a frozen margarita and the machine wouldn't stop – ice was spewing all over the bar like a volcano, I eventually unplugged it. How embarrassing!

I made it through a busy summer Sunday on the beach. "Trial by fire" or whatever that saying is. So now the person who was supposed to relieve me didn't show up. I was about to cry. I don't mind being in the weeds, but not when I don't know what I am doing. The place began to fill up again. Fortunately, there were extra staff and they all pitched in to help through. Finally, the restaurant was closing. I still had a fairly full bar. All of a sudden four police cars pulled up to the front, lights flashing, sirens blaring, they were talking over the PA system. I thought, did I over serve someone? What's this all about? Are they going to raid the place? Man just what I needed. As it turned out the police were just clearing the cars off the beach – no parking after eleven p.m.!

In the end it all worked out. I learned through hard knocks. The owner- Michael, his mother, and the manager really appreciated that I hung in there and didn't abandon ship. I had my choice of shifts all summer long.

LESSON LEARNED: Always hang in there ... but it's nice to know what you're doing.

ASIAN INSPIRED COCKTAILS

Although not listed in the recipes, a splash of apricot brandy gives all of these drinks a nice and somewhat authentic flavor.

Aloha Delight	Brandy, Vodka, Pineapple, Orange Juices
Beachcomber Martini	Light Rum, Dark Rum, Triple Sec, Lemon Juice, Grenadine, Simple Syrup
Love Potion	Light Rum, Banana Liquor, Orange Curacao / Triple Sec, Pineapple Juice Cranberry or Passion Juice. The use of dry ice would give this an amazing special effect.
Mai Tai	Light Rum, Dark Rum, Lime Juice, Orange Curacao, Orgeat (Almond) Mai Tai Mixer (Pineapple, Orange Or Mango)
Zombie	Light Rum, Dark Rum, Apricot Brandy, Triple Sec, Orange Juice, Sour Mix, Grenadine
Fog Cutter	Light Rum, Brandy, Gin, Sour Mix, Orgeat, Orange Juice, Float of Sherry The use of dry ice would give this an amazing special effect.
Head Hunter	Light Rum, Spiced Rum, Crème De Coconut, Passion Fruit Juice

You need to be careful with the dry ice, especially make sure that no pieces gets into the cocktail. I like to use a tea infuser type of strainer. You can enclose a small piece of dry ice and sink it into the cocktail without presenting a danger and it creates a wonderful smoke effect.

Story 3 : NAME YOUR FLAVOR

One summer I got a job on the waterfront of Marblehead. It was a great restaurant with a real chef. When the fishing charters returned, the dock was right out back of the restaurant chef would go down and buy the fish ... and everyone knew that was the special for the night ... how fresh is that?

I only worked the service bar, but the manager was good enough to put five chairs at the bar so I could make extra money. At first, it was difficult to get customers, mostly it was people waiting to be seated. With a little conversation, good service, and great cocktails, I found many of these people were returning and choosing to sit at my service bar rather than a table. Besides, the bar was much more fun and casual. This was working out good for me.

I knew I would have to keep them entertained, and that's part of the job. I developed a game for them (and the kitchen crew). If they gave me a flavor, I would try to make a drink that tasted like it. Usually it would be a dessert. Keep in mind, this was before they had flavored liquors. It is here where I developed my skill and crafted martinis and cocktails like Lemon Meringue, Red Pear, Carrot Cake, Tiramisu, Pancakes and Syrup, Red Velvet, Banana Nut Bread, etc., and of course in the summer - adult shakes.

I had a great gig going that summer. They paid me more as a service bartender and my customers had a great time and were tipping me out at 30% usually. The restaurant closed by 10 p.m. The kitchen crew and I would go out to local places. What a great summer!

After summer, the restaurant slowed down a bit, but my regulars kept coming in to sit at the service bar. This all came to a crashing end right after Thanksgiving. A storm rolled up the coast, and bam! The restaurant got wrecked. Water came right through the floor hatches and just like that the service bar gig was over.

The skills I learned there would be with me for the remainder of my bar years, especially with mixing flavors to create amazing cocktails. It certainly is easier to rely on flavored liquors, but the real fun is being creative in mixing the product. Today, it's more the use of herbs, oils, and smoke to create an effect and it certainly does have its fun aspect also. Makes me think – what's the next trend?

LESSON LEARNED: You need to be creative. Also, all good things come to an end, sometimes it's out of your control.

Story 4: I Can't Drink ... I'll Have a Wine

One of my all-time favorite customer stories is that of Jimmy, a regular at a neighborhood bar. Like many regulars, his social life centered around the bar. He came in at the same time 4 p.m. and drank the same thing- draft lite beer, and left pretty much the same time- 7:30 p.m. Monday through Friday. of course, the weekends were a bit different – we'd see him Saturday mornings about 11 a.m. and he'd stay til about 3 p.m. Sundays only if there was a football or hockey game on. Throw in a couple of takeout orders of food during the week from our restaurant and mixed in with a few Chinese food orders from the place across the street, and his life was complete. Very little can happen that deters a regular from their schedule – to the point where if someone doesn't show up at their regular time the others began to worry.

As much as I tried to keep out of everyone's business, the bartender involuntarily knows a lot. That's because customers have to tell someone their life adventures – and that's usually the bartender. Bartenders are expected, for some reason, to know a little bit about everything, but that just may be because they are usually the sober one in the room, so that makes sense sometimes! Bartenders know about banking, the law, retirement, cars, love, trivia, the current news, history, and so much more.

So one day Jimmy tells me he is going to the doctor, I guess he didn't feel well. of course, most thought he should slow down drinking, or maybe it was the salt in the Chinese food. As it turned out Jimmy needed an operation and had to go the hospital. This was a crisis because the hospital does not have Chinese or fried food ... and no beer for a few days ... this is going to upset his system incredibly.

I knew what day he was going into the hospital and for how long he was going to be staying there. When he didn't show up at his regular time, people began to talk. I reminded them that he had to go into the hospital. and the speculation began, "What's he in for? Cancer?" (he lost some weight), heart attack ("he's been walking slow"), aneurysm ("he's been forgetting things"), maybe back surgery "(he's been slumped over"), and so much more from the rumor mill.

One day Jimmy appears at the bar – a few hours before his regular time, and I knew a few days before he was supposed to be released from the hospital. Jimmy informed me that he was getting bored at the hospital and they weren't really doing anything to help him after his operation. I asked, "Did they release you? How did you get here?"

He said – they didn't release him and that he got up walked out of his room, made it to the front door and hailed a cab. and where do you think the first place he had the cab drop him?... the bar. "Jimmy why did you come here, shouldn't you have gone home and rested?" I asked.

He replied, "Nah I don't have any food in the house. Let me get a chicken parm to go, no pasta, I am trying to lose some weight." I put the order in and told him it would be right out.

Jimmy stood there looking like he was waiting for something. I asked, "You want a water, you don't want a beer, do you?"

"No," he says. "I just got out of the hospital I can't drink already." He thinks for a moment and says, "Get me a white wine." I reminded him he shouldn't be drinking. and his reply was, "I can't drink for a few days, but it's only wine ... it's good for you."

And of course another regular pipes in, "Yeah the wine will relax you, it's on me."

LESSON LEARNED: Sometimes the bartender, no matter how much you try ... you just can't win.

MEDICINAL CURES:

Bartenders are expected to know all the cultural cures and be like an herbal medicine doctor. The patrons of every bar have unique family cures passed on to them by their ancestors. There are so many, I can't list them all but here are a few of my top favorites that really work.

HICCUPS

Take a few lemon slices or wedges, sprinkle some sugar on them (both sides), and a few drops of bitters. Personally, I don't like bitters and think it works just as well if you want to omit the bitters.

Take a few chomps into this mix, and magically, hiccups are gone. I believe it has something to do with the acid of the citrus combined with the sweet sugar

HANGOVER

Sadly, the only cure for this is to not over drink!

BUT, some measures can be taken to lessen the effects of excessive drinking.

Drinking water before you pass out helps to hydrate you, at least you won't get that banging headache when you wake in the morning/afternoon.

To ease the hangover it is common to have a Redeye – which is a mixture of beer and tomato juice. Pretty disgusting but many old timers claim it works. But by the time you drink a Redeye you are already hung over.

UPSET STOMACH

For years people have reached for this cure. Soda water and bitters. No thank you. Although it seems to work for most people that take it. I prefer ginger ale, no ice.

COLD and FLU

There are several concoctions I have listed in the recipes section. and of course I swear by these, as they have guided me through many winters.

If you feel a cold coming on, have two Brandy Alexanders before bed. It provides an uninterrupted sleep and you wake up feeling much better. If that doesn't work, take two more!

If you already have a cold and absolutely need it to go away, my grandfather Charlie would say have a hot tea with honey and Metaxa (Greek Brandy). You know I have to say this usually works.

Story 5: The Guy Who Had No Money

In most restaurants and bars, it is the server's responsibility to manage the table and collect the payment. If the customer leaves without paying, the server has to pay. While most places give the server a pass the first and maybe the second time it happens, after that it is fully on the server and may lead to termination of employment. The point was always explained to me as, "Pay attention to the customer and keep on eye on your tables."

I was fairly new at this restaurant and was working the bar. I heard a commotion in the dining room. The busser came over and told the manager that some guy ran out on his bill. The waitresses (all of whom were over 50 and most in their 60s) chased after the guy, they ran through a busy traffic square, horns were honking and people screaming. They finally caught him across the street.

I asked the manager if I should go and help – meaning I didn't want the ladies to get hurt. He looked at me and said, "No, they got it covered" And, he was completely right. Picture this - Five older women had this dude against the wall, and they were throwing punches like street thugs, until the guy fell to the ground and then they started kicking the crap out of him. When the cops showed up, they had to pull these waitresses off the guy. They told the police that they were willing to press charges. The cop looked at the guy – who at this point, was a total bloody wreck, he looked like a crash dummy that just did a couple of rounds with Tyson, and said, "Geez ladies I think he suffered enough!"

It's amazing what people will do. I had five people come in one night. They ordered some food and drinks and were finishing up. Their friend came with a van, and one by one they were going outside for a smoke, some were getting in and out of the van. Made me very suspicious. of course now they were all outside. No one paid the bill. So, I went outside and they were all getting in the van. I said, "Who's paying the tab?"

They replied, "Oh we'll be right back." I don't think so – I started pulling them out of the van.

"No one's going anywhere until this is paid." As it turns out, they gave this guy their share of payment and he was going to put it the tab on his credit card. But after taking his friends' money, he had no intention of paying and was going to walk out with the cash and stick me with the tab.

His excuse, "Oh I was going to pay when I came back." Stealing is bad enough, stealing from your friends is just disgusting and wrong, what a dirt ball.

A customer I hadn't seen before was sitting at the bar and seemed pleasant enough. He had a few beers, was talking and getting along with some of the regulars. I had no reason to suspect anything. He ordered food and a few more beers. The manager coincidentally brought the food order out and noticed the guy. He pulled me aside and said that he looks like someone that was in last month and had no money to pay his tab with the other bartender. Hmmm. So I went over to the guy, dropped his food off and said, "Sir your tab is getting a bit high – I need a credit card to hold."

Generally, neighborhood places just run a tab and you pay at the end, in the city you have to put up your card to run any amount of a tab. He gave me his card. I went off to the side and input his card... of course it was declined. I went over to him and let him know that the card was declined and told him he'd have to pay cash, for which he replied, " I have no money with me."

"Really, well who's going to pay for what you had?" You know if he came in and said he was short on funds, I would have given him a draft and some pasta. But no way was I going to get stuck paying his bill. I took him in the back and explained some things to him, I took his backpack and told him he'd get it back when he paid the bill. Then I showed him the door and he landed onto the sidewalk.

LESSON LEARNED: Don't try to rip people off ... you get caught eventually and that doesn't turn out good!

Toasts

Bartenders are expected to be able to rally the crowd, whether it's in a restaurant or at home. They are often called upon to lead in a toast and should be ready for any occasion. Here are some to get you started.

May the roof above us never fall in ... and may the friends gathered below it never fall out.

May the best day of your past ... be the worst day of your future.

May you live as long as you want ... and never want for as long as you live.

May you live all the days of your life.

May your troubles be less, and your blessings be more.

There are good ships, and there are wood ships, ships that sail the sea, but the best ships are friendships, and may they always be.

May you be in heaven half an hour before the devil knows you're dead.

Here's to those who wish us well, all the rest can go to hell.

Story 6: *The Lottery Lady*

One of the big differences between neighborhood and city restaurants is that most city restaurants don't have the lottery. I've worked in both and have stories about winners and losers. To be clear, no matter where it is, we only hear about all the money they won. Very rarely does anyone tell you truthfully how much they lost! Most are lucky to break even or have a small loss.

"I won 30 bucks!"

"But Joe you had two $20 tickets!"

There was the guy who won $100,000 – he smartly paid off his mortgage (houses were so much less expensive back then) and car loan and had some left over for him and his wife to enjoy and a bit more to put aside for an emergency fund. Then there was this other guy who won $50,000 on a scratch ticket. He bought a car he didn't need, he and his girlfriend went away on vacation, and he gambled the rest away – leaving him with nothing, especially after his girlfriend took the car and left him!

The restaurant I worked in had a scratch ticket machine, full keno and lottery, and pull tabs. and then of course, there were always football pools, March Madness contests, Superbowl squares, football cards, and so much more.

Anyway, this really nice older lady used to come into the restaurant several times a month. I noticed she always played all kinds of lottery and scratch tickets – I guess it paid off. Because one day we find out she won one million dollars on a $20 dollar scratch ticket – good for her. I thought, "Wow how lucky are you – I wish something like that would happen to me."

I think she took the million over a twenty year period so it would last, still that's $50,000 a year. I just didn't know how much she gambled, until it came to light one day. She came into the restaurant and strategically sat at a table in the middle of the lounge. She got up, walked over to the scratch ticket machine, and bought a bunch of tickets. She wasted no time and began scratching off the tickets as she walked to the lottery station, cashed in her winners, and bought a few keno games. Still scratching, she then walked over to the bar, where she bought twenty pull tabs and started pulling as she walked back over to the ticket machine. She bought more tickets with the money she won and walked over to her table to put in her food order. She was like a tornado, she did the lottery triangle about three times until her food came. She ate while keeping a close eye on keno.

After she finished her meal she cashed in her remaining pull tabs, keno, and scratch tickets. But before she made her way to the cab that was outside to drive her home, she bought another bunch of tickets, probably for the ride home. I was able to ask her though, "Did you win today?"

"Enough to come back another day, but 'they' always win," she said. Well I guess she was realistic about the whole thing. But man, she could have done so much with that million.

LESSON LEARNED: If you can afford to have a good time, then go for it, enjoy yourself ...but remember: the house always wins.

Story 7: *Just a Quickie, She's Waiting in the Car*

To bar regulars, drinking is just part of the day. and the restaurant lounge is like a social club. It's their own little world. Doesn't make them bad people, they're actually very nice and always among the first to donate to charitable causes like fire victims or buy cookies from school groups, etc. But sometimes they just forget the norms of the rest of society.

I was working a weekend day shift. It was normal for the regulars to run in and out (a few times) in the course of a Saturday afternoon for a quick drink between doing their errands. Throw in a little lunch, maybe some keno and those errands become not that bad.

So a regular "popped in" and said, "I'll have a scotch on the rocks, can you make it quick my kid is in the car?"

"Sure." I replied. "How old is your kid?" I asked. (I didn't think she was old enough to drive).

"She's 10," he said. The bar stopped, everyone within hearing distance all looked with condemning stares. It even took me by surprise ... and I don't surprise easily.

It took a moment, but after I recovered, I said, "Buddy I can't give you a drink knowing you're going to get in the car with your 10 year old and drive off. We have limits, and I am just not going to cross that line."

By this time, he noticed that everyone was staring him down. He looked up and said, "You're right what was I thinking? ... I'll be back later" I was just there shaking my head.

But that's the job of a bartender, you're the sober one in the room and as such it's your responsibility to enforce the rights and wrongs. and to make sure that no one gets in trouble or gets hurt ...

LESSON LEARNED: Bartenders and servers sometimes have to be the Common Sense Police.

Paint Night Cocktails – by using edible glitter or pearl dust it gives the paint-like effect.

Paula and I made a cold lobster cocktail appetizer. We shelled the lobster and then reconstructed it.

EVENTS and THEMES:

<u>Medicinal Cocktails:</u>
Brandy Alexander
Honey Ginger Martini
Hot Toddy (Table at 10)
Honey Hot Toddy
Hot – n – Dirty Martini
Irish Coffee
Triple O's

<u>Ski Lodge Warmers</u>
Caribbean Coffee
Chateau Coffee
Gold Rush Hot Cocoa
Hot Cider

<u>From the Bakery</u>
Banana Nut Bread
Black Forest Cake
Carrot Cake
Chocolate Cake Shot
Chocolate Chip Cookie Martini
Gingerbread Martini
Lemon (Pie) Morange Martini
Pistachio Muffin
Strawberry Shortcake
Sugar Cookie Martini

<u>Brunch</u>
Bellini Bar –
      Pear Bellini
      Peach Bellini
      Strawberry Bellini
Banana Nut Bread
French Toast Martini
Mimosa
Pancakes and Syrup
Pistachio Muffin Martini
Sangria
Spicy, Spicy Scary Mary
Tequila Sunrise

<u>Drag Brunch</u>
Between the Sheets
Blow Job Shot
Frisky Whiskey
Fuzzy Navel
Jiggle Juice
Let's Get Kinky
      Mimosa Bar (various fruits and juices)
Nutz and Berries
Piece of Ass
Sex on the Beach
Slippery Nipple
Sweet Nutz
Tie Me to the Bedposts
The Big Banana
Tickle My Coconutz

<u>Fruits and Berries</u>
Appletini
Black Fig Martini
Blueberry Martini
JenBerry Martini
Nutz and Berries
Pomegranate Martini
Red Pear Martini

<u>VFW / Veterans / Memorial Day</u>
B-52
Devil Dog
Green Bean Coffee
Got Your Six
Hurry Up and Wait
Roger That

<u>St. Patrick's Day</u>
Frisky Whiskey
Nutty Irishman
Jamo and Ginger
Kerry Berry
Irish Coffee
Irish Gold
Irish Shake
Irish Mule

<u>Paint Night</u>

These nights are great to bring in new customers, many restaurants are doing them.

By using edible glitter or pearl dust, it gives the cocktail a paint-like shimmer. These can be bought in a crafts store. I suggest the use of mason jar for a good effect.

Mix a margarita or cosmopolitan as you would regularly and add in (I suggest silver) pearl dust. Stir it in until you see the desired effect.

<u>Easter</u>
Bunny Bowl
Peeps Martini
Cotton Tail Marga -Tini

<u>Boston Marathon</u>
Boston Strong
The Finish Line
Heart Break Hill
Run by the Charles

<u>Mother's Day</u>
Apricot Spritz
Cape Cod Mother
Cosmopolitan
Bahama Mama
Pomegranate Martini
Red Pear Martini
Red Sangria

<u>Madi Gras /Carnival / Masquerade</u>
Bayou Bloody Mary
Carnival Punch
Hurricane
Kings Cup Cocktail
Mambo Punch

<u>Cinco De Mayo</u>
Blackberry Margarita
Classic Margarita
Grenada
Jalapeno Cucumber Margarita
Kahlua Sombrero
Pink Paloma
Smoked Chili Margarita
Tequila Sunrise

<u>Kentucky Derby</u>
Bourbon Revival
Churchill Downs Cocktails
Country Lemonade
Front Porch Tea
Kentucky Sunrise
Mint Julep
Southern Comfort Manhattan
Kentucky Mule

<u>Christmas</u>
Black Fig Martini
Candy Cane
Christmas Cocktail
Chocolate Kiss Martini
Eggnog
Maple Whiskey Eggnog
Merry Mimosa
Mistletoe Margarita
Nutcracker
Peppermint Patti
Plum Bellini
Pomegranate Martini
Reese's Cup Hot Cocoa
Snowflake Martini

<u>Calypso Cocktails</u>
Bahama Mama
Bikini Martini
Cubana (Rum and Coca Cola)
Kukoo Kunuku Cocktail
Mambo Punch
Mojito
Strawberry Banana Boat Shake
Tiki Bubbles
Woo Woo

<u>FALL/Thanksgiving</u>
Apricot Rosemary Mimosa
Apple Cider Cinnamon Sangria
Apple Pie
Apple Sauce Martini
Butter Ball
Eve's Temptation
Fall Harvest Sangria
Fall Bellini
Honey Ginger Martini
Intense Ginger Martini
Maple Walnut Old Fashion
Pumpkin Pie Martini
Salted Caramel Martini
Smores Campfire Martini
Washington Apple (Martini)

<u>Halloween</u>
Black Cat Martini
El Diablo
Here's Looking At You Cosmo
Jack – O - Lantern
Love Potion Martini
Love Potion #9
Mounds Bar
Pumpkin Pie Martini
Satin's Whiskers
Snickers Bar
Tootsie Roll
Vampire's Kiss

<u>Italiano / European</u>

Al Capone

Boulevadier

Catrina Cosmo

French Quarter

Godfather

Godmother

Hugo

Italian Flag

Kir

Riviera Cocktail

Sbaliato Milano

Torrino

Venitian Sgroppino

Vito Collins

Story 8: Private Parties

Crafting creative cocktails got me some attention. One of my customers hired me to bartend at her house for a private party. She was part of a group of great people who had all became successful in the trades due to their hard work. They all had beautiful houses, weren't afraid to spend their money, and most importantly, they remembered where they came from. All such nice people who enjoyed partying. Not only did they pay me, but they had me put a tip jar up so their guests could tip me – and they did, very well.

The first party was about 70 people. The men mostly had beers, but the women were all giddy over the cocktails I was making. These folks had so much fun they asked me back the following month to work another party. I brought a helper this time and there were even more people than the first. Eventually I even had to bring a server because they wanted us to pass apps and cocktails. Eventually, their friends were hiring me and my crew to work their parties too. All kinds of occasions – birthdays, anniversaries, Superbowl, graduations, any reason was a good reason!

Most of these parties were catered, they had entertainment, not just a DJ but sometimes a band. The laser light show in the sky was definitely an attention getter. of course, at some point the police would come by. At another yard party, they built an outside bar, tapped the electric from neighbors' houses and had an ice luge, a professional band, and two back up bands. Another had a Superbowl party and the bar in this house was better than any bar I ever worked at, from the bar itself to the beer coolers.

At some point I couldn't keep up with these parties, and as I got older, the liability of it all was becoming too worrisome. Fortunately, they were slowing down a bit too. and they went back to having less people and just doing it themselves. I would stop by occasionally and was eventually phased out.

I am so grateful for the opportunity I had to do these private parties. Professionally, it made me feel accomplished that someone noticed and appreciated, my mixology skills. People are looking, even if you don't know they are. and that's the whole entertainment factor of the business; whether you are making cocktails at a restaurant or making them at home, make them like someone is noticing.

LESSON LEARNED: It's nice to be recognized for what you do, and there are people out there who appreciate you.

VALENTINE ADVENTURE

(she orders) FOR <u>HIM</u>

(he orders) FOR <u>HER</u>

You're my "Old Fashion" Bully Boy
(*Bully Boy Boston whiskey, raw sugar,
soda water, muddled cherry
and orange slice*)

You have me in the "Pama" of
your hand (*Pama pomegranate
liquor, Reyka vodka, and
cranberry juice*)

You hit my "Makers Mark" Manhattan
(*Markers Mark, sweet vermouth*)

I want "smore" of you (smores
martini) (*Vanilla vodka, dark
cream de cocoa, light cream*)

You're my "crown royal" prince
the rocks
(*simply on the rocks*)

Be my "Peppermint Patti" on
martini (*dark cream de cocoa,
vodka, peppermint schnapps*)

I want you to "captain" my cola ship
(*Captain Morgan and coke*)

I go" bananas" nut bread for you
(*cream de banana, hazelnut
liquor, light cream over ice*)

I want to walk down Gin Lane with you
(*Gin lane and tonic*)

I have a "lemon crush" on you
(*Cytron vodka, Lemoncello, fresh
squeezed lemon splash of
lemonade and sprite*)

You drive me "dark and stormy"
(*ginger beer and Gosling black
seal rum*)

You are the "appletini" of
my eye (*vodka, apple pucker
schnapps, splash of sour mix*)

KENTUCKY DERBY TRIVIA

How much is the entrance fee for each horse?

Which Horse and what was the fastest time for the Derby?

What three races make up a Triple Crown? What states are they held in?

What is the name of the race track where the Kentucky Derby is held?

What is the distance of the Kentucky Derby race?

How old are the horses I that race in the Kentucky Derby?

What is the "greatest two minutes in sports?"

What is the official drink of the Kentucky Derby?

What is a female horse called?

What was the name of the last horse to win a Triple Crown?

BONUS: What state do they race the Kentucky Derby?

Kentucky Derby Answers

$25,000 to enter

Secretariat 1:59:30

Kentucky Derby – Kentucky, Preakness – Maryland, Belmont Stakes – NY

Churchill Downs

1 ¼ miles

three years old and under

Kentucky Derby

Mint Julip

Fillie

American Pharoah (2015)

KENTUCKY

ST. PATRICK'S DAY TRIVIA

1. Who was St. Patrick?

An Irish monk who banished snakes from Ireland

A British sailor who was captured by pirates, enslaved in Ireland, and became a monk

An Irishman who warned that the British were coming

2. Why all the three clover green shamrocks?

Three leaf clovers had the power to heal

St Patrick used them to explain the Holy Trinity

They symbolized France, Britain and Ireland for uniting under Catholicism

3. What does Erin Go Brah mean ?

Celebrate spring

Ireland Forever

Luck of the Irish to you

4. How many pints of Guinness are consumed worldwide on St Patrick's Day?

1.2 million

5 million

13 million

5. What item is found at the end of a rainbow?

A bucket of coal

A pot of gold

A cord of wood

6. About what year was St. Patrick born?

500

1807

385

7. St Patrick's Day commemorates ?

The birth of St. Patrick

The death of St. Patrick

The day St. Patrick drove the snakes from Ireland

8. What are the colors of the Irish flag?

Green, white, and orange

Red, white, and green

Blue, white, and red

9. What is the profession of leprechauns?

Blacksmith

Goldsmith

Shoemaker

ANSWERS: a British sailor who was captured by pirates, enslaved in Ireland, and became a monk;

St. Patrick used them to explain the Holy Trinity; Ireland Forever; 13 million; a pot of gold; 385; The death of St Patrick; green, white, and orange; shoemaker

Shorts 1 Continued (The Things You Do Stories)

C. Making a Slow Night Busy

One time I started a carnival game similar to ring toss, I called it Tossing Tuesdays. Customers would get three rubber rings for a dollar and had to get all three rings on the bottles behind the bar. If they did, they would win whatever was in the pot. I only did it on Tuesday night. (I had to figure out a way to make a slow night busy.) I made money because the bar was busy, I just didn't realize how busy it would get. Week after week, no one won, and the pot grew and grew. The first pot got to $1500 before someone finally got all three rings on the bottles. Man I was surprised that it got that high. The second pot was $1200 before someone won. Now word got out and the place was jumping every Tuesday night. People would come down just for Tossing Tuesdays. and restaurant workers would all rush in after they closed their places to get a toss in, so around 1:30 a.m. we were crazy busy. Pots got as high as $1700, eventually the owner found out why his sales were so good on Tuesdays, but that's only because the police called him up. Needless to say, sadly, Tossing Tuesdays had to wind down.

LESSON LEARNED: You have to manage success sometimes!

D. The Jobs You Take

Finding jobs is not always and easy task, especially if the economy is bad. One year I went to so many places looking for summer work. Finally, they hired me at the Hotel Meridien in Post office Square of Boston. It was working at their outside "La Terrace." They hired me as a bartender which paid more because it was essentially a service bar cart. The uniform was very funky to say the least. It started out okay– khaki Bermuda shorts, a white shirt, and white sneakers. Then they gave us a red visor, followed by a red bow tie, and finally they finished it off with red suspenders. We looked like "Yuppie Jepeto gone rogue." I spent most of my time praying that no one I knew walked by. But the money was good. They moved me to a server position and never downgraded my hourly pay. So I was cleaning up at $15 per hour plus tips. In the 1990s that was sweet.

LESSON LEARNED: Sometimes you have to do what you have to do ... to pay the rent.

SHORTS 2 – *The People You Work With...*

Cooks are like adult adolescents, they are in a constant mood change, one minute the nicest people, the next minute totally miserable. They go from intelligent to ...what are you talking about? All in all it's all part of the restaurant business. No matter how big the cut is, it can be wrapped and covered with a rubber glove and the night goes on. One guy I worked with used crazy glue to close a cut on his finger! a customer asked the cook if the tomatoes were vine ripened and he replied yes. I looked at him and he said all tomatoes grow on a vine!

Many years ago, before identity pronouns were woke, I worked with this guy who had one pronoun for everyone. I guess he was way ahead of his time. This guy was the original "Captain Crusty." There were very few people he liked. "Who's the new waitress?... she's an asshole. Does that guy wants a drink?... he's an asshole. Where's the bar back?... he's an asshole." I think asshole was his favorite word and pronoun for all!

Before I had bar experience, I worked the door at this great place on the Boston waterfront. The owners had really cleaned up the place. The food was amazing and the vibe was professional and energetic. On the weekend there were three doormen ..... big (muscle head), medium (me), and small (negotiator). Too funny, every time the small guy would talk to the unruly customer and somehow convinced them to leave, the muscle head would charge over and ask if there was a problem. of course what happened after that was physically persuading the customer to leave!

One of the highlights of my bartender experience came when I got a job at Cheers, Fanuiel Hall. The TV show was no longer but everybody still knew the place. We trained at the original Bull n Finch til we opened. The staff were all young and at 39 years old, it was my first experience at being the "old guy" They opened in summer 2001, shortly after 911 happened – most restaurants had no business but tourists stuck in town would come in because they were comfortable with the place from the TV show. So many times customers would ask, "Do you know my name?" so I would give them a name tag! It was pretty cool – we would have impersonators from the characters of the show come in and sit at the bar – customers got a kick out it. They could take their pictures with Norm and Cliff.

It was a great place and I made money no matter what shift I had. I was fortunate. I always worked til the end so I couldn't go out with the other staff much, by the time I got out, everywhere was closed. These kids would be making about $2000 a week cash, go out after work and spend most of it and at the end of the end of the month they were looking for extra money to pay their rent. Lesson to learn, put some money aside.

As time went on, many of these kids were intrigued by the restaurant business and became managers. They quickly learned that managers don't make tips. As bartenders and servers they were making twice as much as they were as managers with less responsibility. Another lesson – appreciate what you have.

Basic Bar Tools

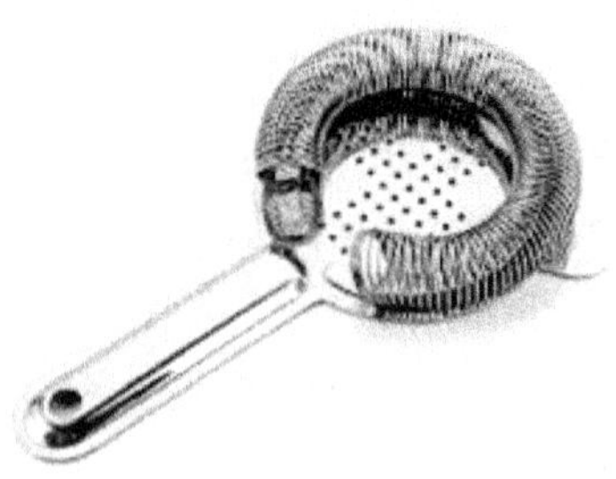

Hawthorne strainer- A metal spring fixed around the edge of the rim rolls inward to fit inside the glass.

Cocktail strainer is normally used to remove ice from mixed drinks as it is poured into service glass. The strainer is placed over the mouth of the shaker or glass in which drinks were prepared.

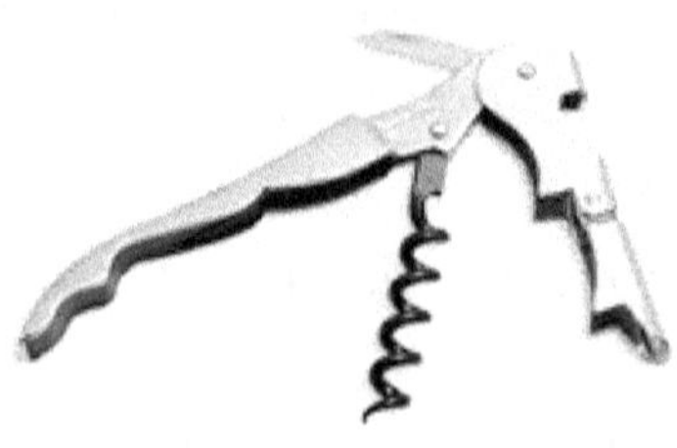

Corkscrew- A most popular corkscrew used by service staff with a knife on one side, nick grip on the other side, and a lever in between, the spiral at one end. This is a crossbar-type lever. It should have the perfect shape for operation.

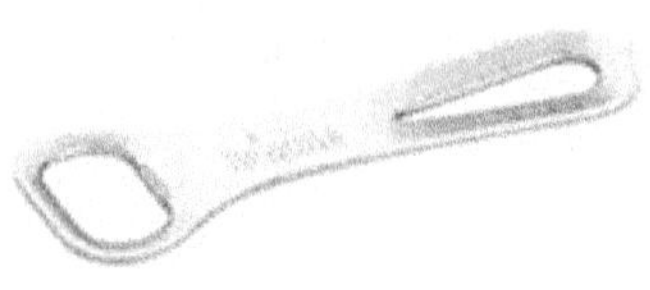

Bottle opener- It is used for the removal of metal bottle caps from the glass bottle jigger.

Bar spoon- It is a long-handled spoon for stirring in mixing bar glass.

 **Muddler-** A cocktail muddler is an essential bar accessory. It is used to mash or muddle fruits, herbs, and spices in the bottom of a glass to release their oils and flavor.

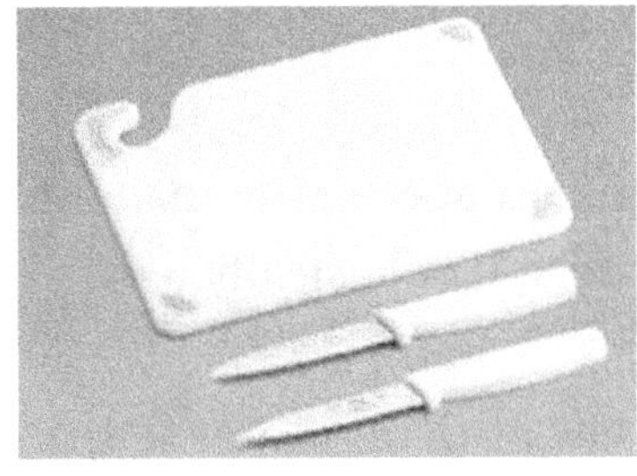 **Knife and chopping board-** A sharp stainless steel knife for cutting citrus fruits as garnishes with a cutting/chopping board with protruding edges to prevent fruit juices from flowing out.

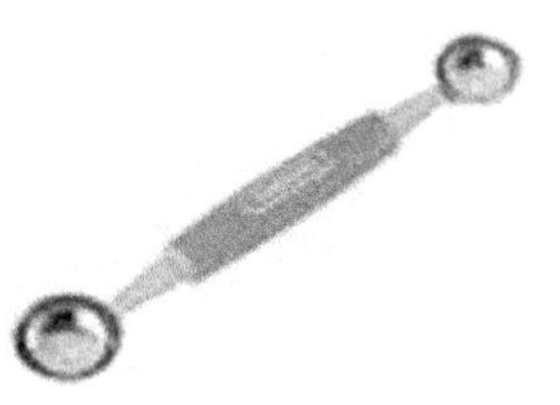 **Melon baller-** Melon ballers are used to make balls of melon from a scoop with a diameter with around 3/8 inch to 1 inch.

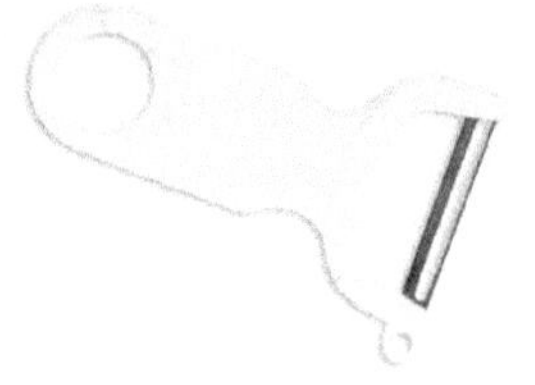 **Peeler-** Used to remove skins of vegetables or fruits, or to create a ribbon of vegetables or fruits.

 **Lemon zester / grater-** It is used for peeling lemon and other vegetable skins. a grater can be used for nutmeg and ginger.

Fruit squeezer- Made of glass, plastic stainless steel manually operated, lever-operated, Fruit squeezes are becoming important in modern bars as fresh fruits are becoming more popular than ever before.

Champagne stopper- It is made of stainless steel, it is basically used to seal the champagne bottle immediately after it is opened, it creates a tight seal on the bottle. The seal gets tighter as the gas from the wine pushes against it.

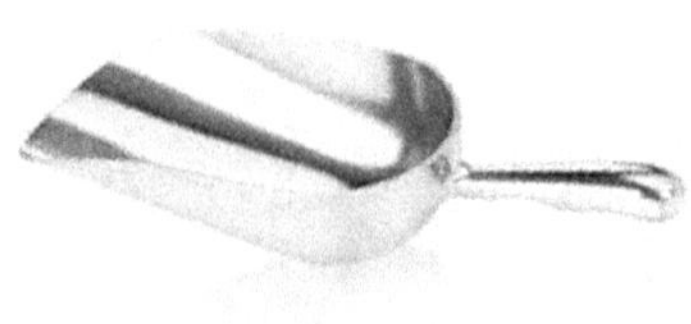

Ice scoop- Ice scoops are used for a variety of ice handling tasks. an ice scoop can be used to fill glassware with ice on the buffet line or at the bar.

Funnel and strainer- Used for straining juices or pouring liquid from one container to the other.

Swizzle Picks- This type of stick is good for olives, garnishes, and also use as food skewers.

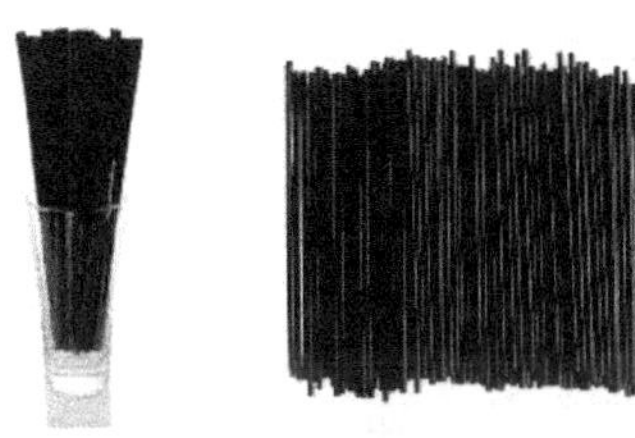

Bar straws and coffee stirrers for cocktails- Both are necessities and the smaller stirrers help to slow down the pace of consumption.

Ice cube sphere tray- Adds a new dimension to your cocktails.

Cocktail torch and smoker- Always be ready to smoke wood or char a garnish.

Bottle Pourer Spouts- Helps to keep the pour consistent and prevents dust from getting into the spirits.

Cocktail Shaker

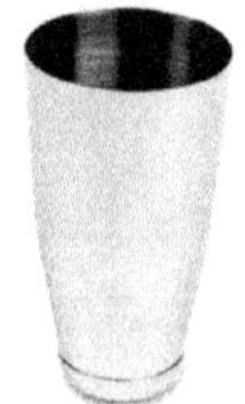

Mixing Cup

About the Author:

I have been in the restaurant business since I was 16 years old. No matter what professional job I had I always worked extra as a bartender either full-time, part-time, summer, or seasonal. Over the years I worked in many places and have accumulated hundreds of cocktail recipes and have met a variety of wonderful, interesting people. Almost every place I worked had signature cocktails and sometimes even the customers had their specialties.

Eventually I opened two successful restaurants. However, after 8 years, I recently sold my restaurants. As I was closing my files I noticed that I have a lot of information to share. It's not just the cocktail recipes, but also quips, toasts, history of some cocktails, medicinal remedies, trends, and more.

The craft of bartending is more than pouring cocktails. The bartender must have a flair for mixology that captures the attention of guests. It's not just shaking the cocktail, but rather getting your guests to be interested in what and how you are mixing. It's being a spirits chemist to combine and execute flavors. Bartending is conveying knowledge and historical facts about the liquor and the cocktail.

Owner:

I was fortunate enough to partner with some friends (Troy Moran and Paula Catalano) and open two restaurants.

Table at 10 (Farm to Table) – North Attleborough, MA
Stella Osteria (Italian) – North Attleborough, MA

Some of the places I worked over the years:
Barney's Bar and Grill - (5 years) – East Boston
Yankee Lounge – (5 years) – Revere
Three Cheers – (3 years) Congress St, Boston
Cheers – (2 years) – Faneuil Hall, Boston
Red Rock Bistro - Swampcott
Jeveli's Restaurant - (24 years) – East Boston

Seasonal and short-term work:
Michael's Seaside – Revere Beach
The Landing – Marblehead
The Chateau – Waltham
Angie's -Revere Beach
The Boston Sail Loft - Boston
La Terrace – Meridian Hotel, Boston
The Witches Brew – Salem
Gourmet Caterers - Boston

Acknowledgments

To my contributing bartender, thank you for adding to this book.

Joe LaMonica, head mixologist at his family restaurant, Vuolo's – Winthrop, MA.

Restaurants have always been a staple in my life since I could remember. I remember late nights missing my mother as she put in long hours at restaurants to help support us with my dad who worked days. I would walk through kitchens at 6 years old and the amazing aromas of food cooking were some of my earliest memories. When I became old enough to drink and had my first cocktail it opened the door of wonder and excitement for me and I have been chasing that same excitement recently.

I have over 15 years of industry experience and 10 of those years as a bartender. All I have learned and all the accomplishments I have had as a bartender came solely from experience. My passion and my love for this came from being there and living it. My love of punk rock and the DIY attitude I have on life is the fuel that keeps my engine revving. I spent years making 100s of terrible unbalanced drinks until I finally learned how to properly shake a martini or the importance of balance. I have and always will be a "working class" bartender. My motto is, "No frill, just thrills." a majority of my cocktails have only one garnish and the reasoning behind this is that I want my guests to focus on flavor, texture, and experience through taste instead of distracting them with theatrics. Great cocktails should be approachable to everyone, not just a specific clientele. That will always be my mission as a drink maker.